LAST LOVE POEMS
of Paul Eluard

TITLES from BLACK WIDOW PRESS

Translation Series

Chanson Dada: Selected Poems by Tristan Tzara
translated & edited by Lee Harwood

Approximate Man & Other Writings, by Tristan Tzara
translated & edited by Mary Ann Caws

Poems of Andre Breton: A Bilingual Anthology
translated & edited by by Jean-Pierre Cauvin and Mary Ann Caws

Last Love Poems of Paul Eluard
translated with an introduction by Marilyn Kallet

Capital of Pain by Paul Eluard
translated by Mary Ann Caws, Patricia Terry and Nancy Kline
(forthcoming)

Love, Poetry by Paul Eluard
translated with an introduction by Stuart Kendall
(forthcoming)

Essential Poems & Writings of Robert Desnos: A Bilingual Anthology
translated & edited by Mary Ann Caws
(forthcoming)

Modern Poetry Series

An Alchemist with One Eye on Fire
Clayton Eshleman
(forthcoming)

New Poet Series

Signal from Draco: Poems of Mebane Robertson
(forthcoming)

and more...

www. blackwidowpress.com

LAST LOVE POEMS OF
PAUL ELUARD

A BILINGUAL EDITION

translated with an introduction by
MARILYN KALLET

BLACK
WIDOW
PRESS

BOSTON, MASS.

Last Love Poems of Paul Eluard
A Bilingual Anthology

Black Widow Press edition, July 2006

Black Widow Press is an imprint of Commonwealth Books, Inc., Boston.
Joseph S. Phillips, Publisher.

All Black Widow Press books are printed on acid-free paper & put into sewn & glued bindings

Black Widow Press
www.blackwidowpress.com

Book design by Nancy C. Hanger

ISBN-13: 978-0-9768449-3-8
ISBN-10: 0-9768449-3-1

Library of Congress Cataloging-in-Publication Data

Eluard, Paul, 1895–1952.
[Derniers poèmes d'amour de Paul Eluard. English & French]
Last love poems of Paul Eluard / translated with an introduction by Marilyn Kallet. — A bilingual ed.
    p. cm.
ISBN-13: 978-0-9768449-3-8 (alk. paper)
1. Eluard, Paul, 1895–1952—Translations into English. 2. Love poetry, French—Translations into English. I. Kallet, Marilyn, 1946– II. Title.

PQ2609.L75D413 2006
843'.912—dc22

2006018525

Prepress & composition by Windhaven Press (www.windhaven.com)
Printed by Thomson-Shore
Printed in the United States

10 9 8 7 6 5 4 3 2 1

For Lou and Heather, always

Contenu

Contents

Acknowledgments to the First Edition

Professor Serge Sobolevitch of the Rutgers Comparative Literature Program offered valuable suggestions on translation for the 1980 edition of this work. Professor Ralph Freedman of Princeton University encouraged me to undertake the project. Poet Miller Williams of the University of Arkansas was the outside reader for the Louisiana State University Press, and I appreciated his generous comments. Beverly Jarrett was a brilliant editor; I was lucky to have had the opportunity to work with her.

Lucien Scheler, Eluard's close friend and editor of both the Seghers and Gallimard editions, was generous in sharing with me his knowledge of Eluard for my introduction. Through a research grant from Hobart & William Smith Colleges I was able to visit Lucien Scheler in Paris in 1979, in order to discuss Eluard's work. He showed me the glossy blue paper that Eluard used for early hand-written drafts. Eluard's pen could glide over such paper effortlessly, as if in a dream.

Cécile Eluard graciously facilitated the production of an English version of *Derniers poèmes d'amour*.

Preface

Translations never keep still. They whisper and nag at the translator: "Don't settle. Bring this closer to the original. Find a more musical phrase. Tighten the line. Stephen Spender nailed this one." Indeed, the admirer of Eluard's poetry will want to seek out Spender's version of the volume, *Le dur désir de durer*, which he translated in collaboration with Frances Cornford. Spender offers the title *The Dour Desire to Endure*; "dour" being less idiomatic than "firm" or "difficult." Spender's lines can sound stodgy at times, though his version of the opening lines of "To Mark Chagall" is elegant: "Donkey or cow cock or horse / Even the shell of a violin." Spender's "even the shell" makes sense of Eluard's line, providing connective tissue.[1] But in reading surrealist poetry, do we want the connections made for us?

By translating the second line, "Toward the hide of a violin," I tried to reinforce the spatial metaphor, and to let "hide" remind the reader of the lively parade of animals in line one. My phrasing includes the "o" sound that holds sway in the French "peau" and "oiseau." Eluard knew that Marc Chagall was going to illustrate the poems for *Le dur désir de durer*. In his playful lines, Eluard was giving Chagall a verbal map, poetical directions. For his part, Chagall was no stranger to objects defying gravity, to the vivid colors of the "couple drenched in its own spring."

How wonderful that Joseph Phillips, of Commonwealth Books, is bringing back into print English translations of French Dadaist and

---

[1] Spender and Cornford, trans. (London: Faber & Faber, 1955). This illustrated out-of-print volume can sometimes be found in rare book collections.

Surrealist poets, under his Black Widow Press imprint. He has given me the opportunity to revisit my translations of Eluard's *Last Love Poems*, first published by Louisiana State University Press in 1980. I am grateful to be able to fiddle with the lines some more. I have turned to poets Jessica Weintraub and Katherine Smith for advice, as well as to Rutgers University Comparative Literature Professors Janet Walker and Steven Walker.

In 1980, I chose to translate the Seghers edition of Eluard's love poems, *Derniers poèmes d'amour.*[2] This slender volume, edited by Eluard's close friend Lucien Scheler, distills four volumes of late love poetry into one book that reads like a long poem. Eluard scholars will want to compare the Seghers edition with the complete poems published by Gallimard; Gallimard offers variants of lines and of sequences of poems. Eluard published two versions of *Corps mémorable*, in 1947 and 1948; the first with punctuation, the second without. I like the sleek look of the second edition, reprinted by Seghers, whereas the punctuated Gallimard edition makes Eluard sound sedate, more like Baudelaire than Breton.[3]

In the years since I first translated Eluard, two particularly engaging books in English have helped to elucidate the poet's relationships. Eluard's *Letters to Gala* gives us a portrait of his passionate devotion to his first wife, whom he met at a tuberculosis sanitarium when both were seventeen years old.[4] They were married in 1917, and a year later Gala gave birth to their daughter Cécile. In 1924, when Gala left him for Max Ernst, Eluard pulled "a Rimbaud," and took off for the Far East. Gala and Ernst followed him, and their adventures are chronicled, with gorgeous illustrations of Ernst's artwork, in *Ghost Ships: A Surrealist Love Triangle.*[5]

Eluard's letters to Gala reveal that he remained devoted to her throughout his life. Her leaving at first tormented him. Yet his letters never express recriminations, only love and longing. Gala later entered a relationship with Salvador Dali, whom she married. Eluard himself

---

[2]   Editions Seghers (Paris, 1973).

[3]   Eluard, Oeuvres complètes, eds. Marcelle Dumas and Lucien Scheler (Paris: Editions Gallimard, 1968), 121–127.

[4]   Eluard, Letters to Gala (New York, Paragon House, 1989).

grew more devoted to his second wife, Nusch, whom he had married in 1934. In his March 1935 letter to Gala, Eluard explains the deepening of his relationship to Nusch: "She is for me, as Dali is for you, an entirely loving and devoted being, perfect."[6]

Enduring two years in hiding together during the war brought Nusch and Eluard closer. After Nusch's sudden death in 1947, Eluard was so grief-stricken that he was unable to write to Gala. On March 10, 1947, Cécile wrote to her mother, "I see my father fairly often . . . he isn't getting over Nusch's death and I don't know what to do to help." The poems in *Le temps déborde* (*Time Overflows*) speak for themselves about the quality of Eluard's love and grief. The ensuing poems sing of sadness and return to life, to a third marriage, with Dominique. Eluard's poetry conveys to us a passionate temperament, and expresses a determination to love, past war, past grief--to reinvent himself, to create in poetry the "human door" that opens both a magical world of invention and a "common exchange between us."

---

[5] Robert McNab, *A Surrealist Love Triangle* (New Haven: Yale, 2004).

[6] *Letters to Gala*, 204.

Introduction

Paul Eluard (1895–1952) is considered to be one of France's most important poets. Until recently, it has been difficult to get a hold of whole books of Eluard's poetry in English translation.[1] We think that we know Eluard's poetry, but without more of the body of work accessible to us, it is difficult to grasp the plot or mythos in the poetry, and impossible to trace the poet's evolution over decades. For too long we have been under the misconception, propagated at least in part by academia, that Eluard is to be considered only as a Surrealist, and enjoyed or dismissed as such. But Eluard's poetic activity was divided into two stages: his exploratory work in poetics as a Dadaist and then as a Surrealist (1919-1938), and his more traditional yet modern post-Surrealist work from 1938-1952. This latter period was for Eluard a time of passionate love and intense political involvement. The marvelous books of *Last Love Poems (Derniers poèmes d'amour)*, composed during 1946-1951, give us an idea of Eluard's technical mastery as a mature poet, enabling us to participate in the universality of his poetry, and to understand why he is held in international esteem.

---

[1] Of the more than one hundred collections of Paul Eluard's poetry published in French, only one volume of English translation was readily available in 1980, *Uninterrupted Poetry*, by Lloyd Alexander (New York: New Directions, 1973, rpt. Greenwood, 1977). Since then, Alexander and Cicely Buckley have translated *Ombres et Soleil/Shadows and Sun: Selected Writings of 1913-1952* (Durham: Oyster River Press, 1996). In 2006, Black Widow Press (Boston) will publish *Capital of Pain (Capitale de la douleur)*, translated by Mary Ann Caws, Patricia Terry, and Nancy Kline, and in 2007, *Love, Poetry (L'amour la poésie)* translated by Stuart Kendall.

Language That Sings

"Language that sings, language charged with hope even when it is desperate"[2]—this is the poetic language that Paul Eluard required, and that he offers us in *Last Love Poems*. For Eluard, poetry is possibility looking for a human voice: it is "man, singer, a lonely bird," who opens the volume of love poems that we have in hand, whose song gives birth to the world. (Inspired by Eluard's lyricism, the French composer Francis Poulenc has set many of Eluard's poems to music, including "To Marc Chagall," the first poem of *Last Love Poems*.) The poet's voice cannot be stifled, for it sustains the community as well as the writer. According to Eluard, poetry is always "the bearer of a profound intelligence, of reason rooted in instinct, in sensitivity, in the need to live."[3] If the poet invokes death, he or she does so "only out of spite."

The love which illumines the verses of Eluard's late poetry takes different forms as the poet is confronted by sudden personal tragedy in 1946 and must find his way back to the living through language. The music of each book differs. There are poems in The *Firm Desire to Endure* that seem to play jigs ("To Marc Chagall"); songs that sound more solemn, wedding hymns ("Order and Disorder of Love"); other poems sing the blues ("Here"). In *Time Overflows* there are poems of grief that have barely crossed the border into speech but, once uttered, present not merely a personal voice, but a human voice as rich with sorrow and as disciplined in its expression as ancient tragic verse. In *Memorable Body* there is sensual music, and *The Phoenix* offers us a fervent, "lively air" of reawakened love. Eluard was fifty-six at the time of the composition of *The Phoenix* (1951); he brings all of his experience and technical skill to bear to make the poems flow easily toward the reader. Having found love again at this time in his life, the poet conveys to us a sense of steadiness and affirmation at the heart of the marvelous.

---

[2] Eluard, *Oeuvres complètes*, ed. Marcelle Dumas and Lucien Scheler (Paris: Editions Gallimard), II, 931.

[3] *Oeuvres complètes*, I, 931–32.

Together the four books tell a personal and mythic story: of Eluard's love for his wife Nusch and for a life graced by their love; of shock and grief over his wife's sudden death; of purgatory, the life of the senses renewed through friendship and sensual love; of the rebirth of the couple and community through a new marriage to Dominique. The pattern is Orphic, expressing a drama of descent from bliss into extreme suffering, then reemergence into strength and oneness. But the pattern is not arbitrary—for Eluard had a will and a passion for renewal. While he did not seek grief and solitude, he was determined to begin again with "new and pure eyes" after each confrontation with the depths of the abyss.

The important books of *Last Love Poems*, collected posthumously by Seghers in 1963, were selected from among other works written by Eluard in the late 1940s and early 1950s. The Surrealist poets, among whom Eluard was a moving force in the nineteen-twenties and thirties, delighted in seeing the surprises, unexpected meanings, and hidden poetry that juxtapositions could create. The four books juxtaposed against one another as we find them dramatize a plot and a marvelous poetic continuity that underlies Eluard's late work.[4]

Each Book as a World

The mood of *The Firm Desire to Endure* (1946) is predominantly one of joy and innocence, for the poet takes renewed delight in seeing Paris and the world around him that has been freed from Nazi occupation. In these poems Eluard luxuriates in the bonds that he shares with his wife Nusch, whose love has provided a source and symbol of

---

[4] The order of poems in *The Firm Desire to Endure* (*Le dur désir de durer*) has been rearranged from the slightly erroneous 1963 Seghers edition, to match the first edition published by Bordas in 1946. For the rest, we have been able to follow Seghers and stay close to the original order of poems. Two poems, "Écrire dessiner inscrire" and "La petite enfance de Dominique," have been omitted from the fourth book, *The Phoenix* (*Le phénix*).

cohesiveness against the destructiveness of war. Eluard rejoices as well with tenderness for the French people, his community, which has survived the disaster. The poems are more than a sigh of relief, they are songs and celebrations of relief; yet all the while the verses retain a memory of the war's shattering power. Like Blake's *Songs of Innocence*, the poems of *The Firm Desire to Endure* contain traces and omens of a world of experience and destruction. There are still "waves of walls and the absent air of children" to remind us of the misery caused by the Second World War. Though Eluard's songs are apparently simple, they are never foolish in their joyfulness. The "firm desire to endure" is also a difficult desire to endure: it is hard to sustain hope in a time when so much has been devastated.

The first poem in this series of love poems is to Marc Chagall. It is fitting that the book opens with a song that transmits the poet's love of seeing. What we see is renewal: fresh, bright colors of gold, green, red and blue tint this poem, and set the tone for this book of inner brightness and renewed hope. In the way of the best Surrealist collaborations, Eluard wrote the poem in a style imitative of Chagall's lyricism and playfulness in painting (while knowing that the poem would be illustrated by Chagall in the first edition). Animals come dancing in on the first line; man is not far behind, and he, too, is a dancer with his woman. The buoyancy of the poem defies gravity and sets the stage for gestures of ascent and return that are reenacted throughout Eluard's poetry. Eluard wanted his poems to be heard, sung, painted, danced, to be enjoyed to the utmost by his readers.

The most striking of the books, perhaps one of the most beautiful and sad works in French poetry, is *Time Overflows* (1947).[5] These poems require all of Eluard's mastery and control to express his overwhelming grief after Nusch's death. Here is an honest language, stripped of any verbal or emotional pretense. Paul Eluard met Nusch in 1930, and loved her from the start. They shared years of passionate, devoted marriage which freed Eluard to write with lightness and vigor. Love for Nusch helped Eluard to create a world in poetry teeming with generative

---

[5] On June 16, 1947, under the pseudonym of Didier Desroches, Eluard published *Le temps déborde* in a limited edition for his friends.

power, enabled him to embrace the world in his poetry. Nusch's sudden death of a cerebral hemorrhage on November 28, 1946, shocked the poet into a state of grief bordering on madness. In his sorrow, Eluard even became jealous of the dead.

In *Time Overflows* Eluard expresses a state of stasis, dismemberment, as he is severed from his wife and from himself: "My eyes tore themselves from your eyes / They lose their confidence they lose their light." Eluard finds himself in an "extended desert" where time and space no longer promise growth, but threaten him with a terrible emptiness. The poet is never sentimental in these poems of grief; he states his feelings directly, as facts: "I was so close to you that I am cold near others."

Yet the last poem in the book is one of hope, for "the firm desire to endure" pushes the poet toward life again, toward life-giving sources. By temperament Eluard could not tolerate solitude; in his sorrow he turned all the more to a vision of intimacy and community for solace:

> We will not reach the goal one by one but by two
> Knowing ourselves by two we will all know each other
> We will all love each other and our children will laugh
> At the dark legend where a lonely one cries.
>
> ("Our Life")

During this time of crisis Eluard's friends sustained him with their love and presence. Jacqueline was everything to him at this time—mother, lover, friend—and she kept the poet alive with warmth that distracted him from his torment. The poems in *Memorable Body* (1948)[6] sing of the return of the poet's senses; the language has to it an atmosphere of lubricity, evoking the "sleek and humid spectacle" of the lover's body. Time, which had tortured Eluard in his grief, again holds the possibility of pleasure: seeing revives as Eluard views his lover:

---

[6] Eluard published two editions of *Corps mémorable*, in 1947 and in 1948. The second edition augmented the first, and all of the poems are included here. The first edition was published under the pseudonym of Brun.

I see you nude knotted arabesque
Hand slack at each turn of the clock
Sun slow along the length of the day
Plaited rays braids of my pleasures
                    ("Between the Moon and the Sun")

However, *Memorable Body* is also a book of conflict, for the memory of Nusch keeps calling the poet away from life.

In 1949, while in Mexico for a World Peace Congress, Eluard met Dominique, whom he was to marry in 1951, just one year before his death. The poems of *The Phoenix* (1951) are a tribute to Dominique, and to love's power to restore a man's life. Images of the community return with the return of personal love and commitment; the networks of communication that make the world a habitable place are re-created for Eluard. Once more "the walls of the house have common skin." *The Phoenix* is studded with suns and images of light and morning. "I look at you and the sun grows." Night's sorrows dissolve in the warmth of Dominique's love. "It is the beginning of the world."

Yet one might find traces in *The Phoenix* of Eluard's premonition of his death. There is a tone of urgency in "Seascape" as Eluard sings, "Outside the boats are in low tide / Everything must be said in a few words." In these lines Eluard sums up his sense of responsibility to his craft. The poet knows that he speaks to and for many, and that he must do so with the greatest economy. For we are needy of the warmth and emotional riches of poetry: "the sea is cold without love."

Style and Philosophy of Poetry

The accessibility of Eluard's late poetry is a sign of his respect for the reader. His poems do not turn in and round upon themselves in glorification of their own form, but make a fraternal gesture toward the reader. The purpose of the love poems is to communicate, to share feeling and the joys of perception through music. Eluard frequently uses the word *nu*, or naked, in his poetry—like the lover's body the poet's language "simplifies itself" in its bareness. The banishment of excesses and eccentricities of style helps the poet to reach a wide audience.

Eluard usually relies on a basic vocabulary, one in common usage. We are not distracted by the words of Eluard's poetry and therefore through their combinations words are free to deliver up the poems' incantatory power. As Gide expresses it, "Incantation (in the poems of Eluard . . .) is obtained exclusive of and in spite of the meaning of words. . . . Eluard retains only their incantatory power. . . . Thus he forms around words a sort of diffuse halo; their contours are rainbowed."[7]

Even in the incantations the poet's statements are direct, spoken with the rhythm of speech or song, conveyed in the syntax of the ordinary sentence. The refrain, such as that used in "I Love You," is one of the basic devices of poetry, and as such is not only incantatory but is a sign of a common experience: the refrain repeats and rehearses the poet's feelings so that the reader understands and participates in the story, in a progression of emotion toward joy. The "transparent clarity" of Eluard's poetry and the apparent ease of his style are linked to his attitude toward poetry and society. Eluard prefaced one of his early books of poetry, *The Animals and Their Men* (1920), by asking for an "honest power" to return to the poets: "And the displeasing language which suffices to the garrulous, language as dead as crowns to our equal brows, let us reduce it, transform it into a charming language, a true one, of common exchange between us."[8] It is Eluard's goal to use language as a medium of common exchange, to enable us to share "the wheat and the bread of beauty."

In his critical writings Eluard chose to repeat Lautréamont's dictum that "poetry must be made by all. Not by one."[9] The revolutionary power of poetry is that it enables us to share the world in language. The solitude and alienation of the poet are a thing of the past; "the lonely one who cries" is only a legend as the poet expresses the rapports among people in society. Poetry has no actuality, no flesh

---

[7] Andre Gide, "Sur une définition de la poésie," *Poésie* 41, no 3 (March, 1941).

[8] *Oeuvres complètes*, 1, 37.

[9] *Ibid.*, 514.

and blood for Eluard, until the moment when there is "reciprocity," when the reader and the poet are equal and equally content with their lives. Though Eluard theorized about the need for a common language in poetry as early as 1920, it was not until the late thirties that his poetry began to assume traditional forms with frequency. Eluard's seeking to make his poetry clearer to the reader through a common form corresponds to a strengthened political commitment in his later years.

Eluard's Poetic Development in Historical Context

Though Eluard never sought to distort language in his poetry, his early Dadaist and Surrealist works are by their nature experimental and therefore less direct than later poems such as *Last Love Poems*. These love poems represent the summation of a career; they are the result of a poetic evolution that took place over thirty years. Historical circumstances as well as constant experimentation with the craft of poetry helped to reinforce in Eluard a commitment to poetry that would be less hermetic than Surrealist poetry.

In 1919 Eluard began to collaborate with André Breton, Louis Aragon, and Phillipe Soupault on their dadaist projects, working along with the Romanian Tristan Tzara, who had begun the Dadaist movement in Zurich in 1916. When Tzara and the pure rebellion of Dadaism were abandoned for Surrealism in 1922, Eluard continued to work with the Surrealist group, to be one of its most dynamic and influential members until 1938. Probably Eluard's love of fellowship and artistic cooperation led him to work with the Surrealists as much as did his love of the marvelous in poetry. For Eluard could count not only the poets mentioned above as his friends in those early years of Surrealism (he quarreled with Aragon in 1932, the two men were reconciled through their work in the Resistance in 1942), but also René Char, Max Ernst, and Picasso, who was a close friend of Eluard's to the end of his life.

Eluard's collaboration with Benjamin Péret on strange and spontaneous "proverbs" (1925); his project with André Breton and René

Char, *To Slow Work Down* (1930); and the collaboration with Breton
on *The Immaculate Conception* (1930) produced some astonishing texts
and taught Eluard useful techniques for his later poetry: techniques
of juxtaposition of images and phrases; enumeration of surprising
images; free association and play with sounds and meanings. With
its automatic writing, Surrealism encouraged Eluard's fluidity of style;
his lines move with the ease of a sleepwalker. For Eluard, as for his
companions, Surrealism was a means to explore the unknown, to mine
the unconscious and the world of dreams. But for Eluard these new
resources were also to be used toward the building of an aestheti-
cally pleasing language, a language which could be an end in itself
if its beauty reached people.

With his capacity to love one woman "for all the women he did not
love," Eluard inspired the Surrealists with his vision of love, and for
the time of his most intense involvement with the Surrealists Eluard
and his friends created among themselves a reciprocal language. But
experimental texts such as *The Immaculate Conception*, while they may
contain revelations for psychology and display dazzling imagery, are
not easy to understand. In fact, these writings are not meant to be
grasped: "There are walls here that you will not cross." [10]

Eluard's early poems can be sonorous and measured, as in *Capital of
Pain* (1926), or delicate, in *Immediate Life* (1932): "The doors open the
windows unveil." But many of the poems in the early books also seem
elliptical and cryptic. Without connectives to hold the lines together,
there is fragmentation ("Everything thrown everywhere / Everything
seemed disparate" [11]). Often verbs are implicit or missing altogether;
for better or for worse the subject is a mystery. Poems can degener-
ate into lists: "Slaps cries bumps / Buds of rage rinds of laughter." [12]
Besides being difficult to understand, longer poems such as "Like an
Image" from *Love Poetry* (1929) are weighted down with images, with
the expected unexpected.

---

[10] *Ibid.*, 308.

[11] *Ibid.*, 387.

[12] *Ibid.*

Eluard was not satisfied to keep up the walls of imagery in his poetry. Surrealism was the "absolutely modern" means of expression of his day, and Eluard had made his apprenticeship in poetics through his work with Surrealism. But he extended himself and his work beyond it. Most critics of Eluard's work agree that by 1936 the poet had, as an act of conscience, become a more public writer, combining his political and external life with his love poetry in a new amalgam. As Eluard says in *Handrail* (1936), his verses gained by having to become more "attentive / to the people whom he reunites."[13]

In the summer of 1936 the Fascist forces began to war on the people of Spain; Federico García Lorca was shot in Granada. Sensitive to the world around him, Eluard could not help but be affected by the Spanish Civil War. In his famous poem "The Victory of Guernica" (*Natural Course*, 1938) he sent to the besieged people of Spain and to the troubled people of Europe clear messages of support and hope. In that same year, Eluard made his decisive break with Surrealism, and he broke with André Breton, whom he never saw or spoke to again. Under the pressure of circumstances Eluard drew near once again to the Communist party, which he had joined in 1926 and then became distant from in the 1930s. In 1942 he asked to rejoin the party. The word *hommes*, meant as a sign for "people" rather than just for "men," recurs in the poetry of this period like a refrain, for Eluard was writing to express the feelings of many, and to rally the people against fascism. As we can see from Last Love Poems, Eluard's communism is not obtrusive in his poetry, but implicit in the love he expresses for people and in the vision of a fresh world that he wants to share with them.

During the Occupation (1942-1944) Eluard went into hiding in the rue Tournon at the home of Lucien Scheler, and from there became the director of the northern zone of the National Committee of Writers (Aragon directed the southern zone), creating a center of the intellectual Resistance in Paris. Eluard's book *Poetry and Truth* (1942), published by the clandestine press Editions La Main à Plume, appeared

---

[13] *Oeuvres complètes*, II, 485.

in England (in translation) and in Algeria, and was parachuted by R.A.F. forces over occupied French territories. Included in this book, the famous poem "Liberty," with its incantatory song of freedom, had tremendous popular impact and was widely memorized. Motivated by his feeling for Nusch—"Liberty" was at first written for her—Eluard spoke clearly and directly to the French people.

Eluard did not give up his love of the marvelous in the late poems, as we can see from the most Surrealistic poem in *Last Love Poems*, "I Still Live," with its "blue globules of a discolored world," its dreamlike imagery, or from the "rainbowed" surfaces of "To Marc Chagall." But the poems, the "human trellis between us," always return to earth, to the people who live within them. The last love poems have content, not just imagery; they tell of love and of a will to keep living.

More than a quarter of a century after Eluard's death, we can now see that he was not only a Surrealist innovator but also a great poet, whose life impressed upon him the need to communicate with his society. Eluard is a love poet, a poet of dreams and of the inner life responsive to the external world. His passion to create poetry that includes people and can be shared, a language "of one and two, of everyone," that keeps extending itself, is a kind of Whitmanesque devotion to language that joins people and sings their lives. It is not with Breton, but with Neruda that we should compare Eluard, in terms of his stature as a poet and of his impact on his audience. Neruda admired Eluard greatly for his "passionate lucidity."[14] Eluard's poetry, like Neruda's, became a public language and a public good. The inner action of Eluard's poetry, the "firm desire to endure," reminds us to listen for "language charged with hope even when it is desperate" among our best contemporary poets.

—Marilyn Kallet

---

[14] See Pablo Neruda, *Memoirs*, trans. Hardie St. Martin (New York: Ferrar, Straus and Giroux, 1977), 277-78.

I.
Le dur désir de durer

I.
(The Firm Desire to Endure)

A Marc Chagall

Ane ou vache coq ou cheval
Jusqu'à la peau d'un violon
Homme chanteur un seul oiseau
Danseur agile avec sa femme

Couple trempé dans son printemps

L'or de l'herbe le plomb du ciel
Séparés par les flammes bleues
De la santé de la rosée
Le sang s'irise le coeur tinte

Un couple le premier reflet

Et dans un souterrain de neige
La vigne opulente dessine
Un visage aux lèvres de lune
Qui n'a jamais dormi la nuit.

To Marc Chagall

Donkey cow cock or horse
Toward the hide of a violin
Man singer a single bird
Nimble dancer with his woman

Couple drenched in its spring

Gold of grass the lead of sky
Separated by blue fires
Of the blush of dew
The blood pearls the heart tolls

A couple the first gleam

And in an underground of snow
The opulent vine designs
A face with lips of moon
That has never slept at night.

Par un baiser

Jour la maison et nuit la rue
Les musiciens de la rue
Jouent tous à perte de silence
Sous le ciel noir nous voyons clair

La lampe est pleine de nos yeux
Nous habitons notre vallée
Nos murs nos fleurs notre soleil
Nos couleurs et notre lumière

La capitale du soleil
Est à l'image de nous-mêmes
Et dans l'asile de nos murs
Notre porte est celle des hommes.

By a Kiss

Day the house and night the street
The street musicians all play
To the end of silence
Under the black sky we see clearly

The lamp is filled with our eyes
We inhabit our valley
Our walls our flowers our sun
Our colors and our light

The capital of the sun
Is in our image
And in the shelter of our walls
Our door is that of men.

Ordre et désordre de l'amour

Je citerai pour commencer les éléments
Ta voix tes yeux tes mains tes lèvres

Je suis sur terre y serais-je
Si tu n'y étais aussi

Dans ce bain qui fait face
A la mer à l'eau douce

Dans ce bain que la flamme
A construit dans nos yeux

Ce bain de larmes heureuses
Dans lequel je suis entré
Par la vertu de tes mains
Par la grâce de tes lèvres

Ce premier état humain
Comme une prairie naissante

Nos silences nos paroles
La lumière qui s'en va
La lumière qui revient
L'aube et le soir nous font rire

Au coeur de notre corps
Tout fleurit et mûrit

Sur la paille de ta vie
Où je couche mes vieux os

Où je finis.

Order and Disorder of Love

To open I will cite the elements
Your voice your eyes your hands your lips

I am on earth would I be here
If you were not also

In this bath that faces
The sea of sweet water

In this bath that flame
Has built in our eyes

This bath of happy tears
Into which I have entered
By the virtue of your hands
By the grace of your lips

This first human state
Like a dawning prairie

Our silences our words
Light which goes
Light which returns
Dawn and evening make us laugh

At the heart of our body
All flowers and ripens

On the straw of your life
Where I lay my worn bones

Where I end.

Le mouvement du soir

Petit feu d'occasion miroir
Abeille et plume détachée
Loin de la gerbe des rues
Des familles des retraites

Devant tes yeux petit feu
Qui soulève tes paupières
Et qui passe et qui s'en va
Dans la soir limpide et frais

Vers d'autres yeuxs tout pareils
De plus en plus assombris
De plus en plus achevés
De moins en moins existants.

The Movement of Evening

Small fire sale mirror
Bee and feather unbound
Far from the sheaves of streets
Of families of retreats

Before your eyes small fire
Which raises your lids
And which passes and goes
In the clear cool evening

Towards other eyes just the same
Darker and darker
More and more perfect
Less and less existent.

Même quand nous dormons

Même quand nous dormons nous veillons l'un sur l'autre
Et cet amour plus lourd que le fruit mûr d'un lac
Sans rire et sans pleurer dure depuis toujours
Un jour après un jour une nuit après nous.

Belle

Belle tu vas briser en t'endormant la chaîne
Qui lie la plume de minuit au plomb des cendres
Le corps mort à la bête qui bondit en songe
Parmi les herbes et les feuilles confondues
L'étendue verte a des charbons qui boivent l'ombre

Belle tu recevras la nourriture insigne
Par les yeux au fuseau des veines et des nerfs
Lumière intime flamme et frisson du matin
Il est très tard ferme les yeux demain rayonne
Demain mieux qu'aujourd'hui tu connaîtras le monde

Belle d'un jour et de toujours et de partout
Ta faiblesse et ta force ont la même parure
O bien aimée de tous et bien aimée d'un seul
En silence ta bouche a promis d'être heureuse
Au coeur de tous au coeur d'un seul à notre coeur.

Even When We Sleep

Even when we sleep we watch over one another
And this love heavier than the ripe fruit of a lake
Without laughter and without tears has lasted forever
Day after day a night after us.

Belle

Belle while sleeping you will break the chain
Which ties the pen of midnight to the lead of ashes
The dead body to the beast which leaps in dream
Among the confused grasses and leaves
The green plain has coals which drink darkness

Belle you will receive worthy sustenance
From eyes at the spindle of veins and nerves
Intimate light flame and shiver of morning
It is very late close your eyes tomorrow glows
Tomorrow you will know the world better than today

Belle of one day and of always and everywhere
Your weakness and your force have the same adornment
O beloved of all and beloved of one
In silence your mouth promised to be happy
In the heart of all the heart of one in our heart.

Dit de l'amour

I

Notre silence fera taire la tempête
Assagira le feuillage profond

J'ai dans les mains deux mains abandonnées

II

Ce bateau s'enfonçait à jamais dans la brume

De loin en loin qui dit la haine
De proche en proche dit l'amour

III

Les yeux d'air vif souveraine innocente
Les seins légers elle riait de tout

Et la mer dispersa le sable de son trône.

Lay of Love

I

Our silence will quiet the storm
Tame the deep leaves

In my hands I have two surrendered hands

II

This boat penetrated endlessly into the fog

Far farther the one who says hate
Close closer says love

III

Eyes of bright air innocent queen
Light breasts she laughed at everything

And the sea dispersed the sand of her throne.

Dit de la force de l'amour

I

Le soleil dur comme une pierre
Raison compacte vigne fauve

Et l'espace cruel est un mur qui m'enserre

II

Dans ce désert qui m'habitait qui m'habillait

Elle m'embrassa et en m'embrassant
Elle m'ordonna de voir et d'entendre

III

Par des baisers et des paroles
Sa bouche suivit le chemin de ses yeux

Il y eut des vivants des morts et des vivants.

Lay of the Power of Love

I

The sun hard like a stone
Compact reason tawny vine

And cruel space is a wall that entraps me

II

In this desert that inhabited me that clothed me

She embraced me and embracing me
She ordered me to see and hear

III

By kisses and words
Her mouth followed the path of her eyes

There were the living the dead and the living.

Dit d'un jour

Pour cerner d'un peu plus de tendresse ton nom

La rue était absurde et la maison amère
Le jour était glissant la nuit était malade.

De détail en détail

à Elsa Triolet

A l'heure du réveil près du nid de la terre
Un rayon de soleil creuse un trou pour la mer

Trempée d'aube une feuille ourle le paysage
Naïve comme un oeil oublieux du visage

Et le jour d'aujourd'hui saisissant les dormeurs
Rejette dans la nuit leurs ombres de dormeurs.

Tale of a Day

To surround your name with a little more tenderness

The street was absurd the house bitter
The day was slippery the night was sick.

From Detail to Detail

To Elsa Triolet

At the hour of awakening near the earth's nest
A ray of sun drills a hole for the sea

Dipped in dawn a leaf hems the landscape
Naïve as an eye oblivious of the face

And the day of today seizing sleepers
Casts off in the night their shadows of sleepers.

Un seul sourire

Un seul sourire disputait
Chaque étoile à la nuit montante
Un seul sourire pour nous deux

Et l'azur en tes yeux ravis
Contre la masse de la nuit
Trouvait sa flamme dans mes yeux

J'ai vu par besoin de savoir
La haute nuit créer le jour
Sans que nous changions d'apparence.

A Single Smile

A single smile contested
Each star in the rising night
One smile for us two

And the blue in your delighted eyes
Against the mass of the night
Found its fire in my eyes

I saw through the need to know
Deep night create day
Without our changing shape.

Corps idéal

Sous le ciel grand ouvert la mer ferme ses ailes
Aux flancs de ton sourire un chemin part de moi

Rêveuse toute en chair lumière toute en feu
Aggrave mon plaisir annule l'étendue

Hâte-toi de dissoudre et mon rêve et ma vue.

Ideal Body

Beneath the wide open sky the sea folds its wings
At the flanks of your smile a path leaves from me

Dreamer all in lustrous flesh all aflame
Aggravate my pleasure cancel the expanse

Hasten to dissolve both my dream and my sight.

De solitude en solitude vers la vie

En ce temps-là, une extraordinaire résignation avait suc-
cédé à la terreur et à révolte. Saintes et martyrs pullulaient.

I

Je suis douce avec les forts
Je suis faible avec les doux
Je sais les mots qu'il faut dire
Pour n'inspirer que l'oubli

Je suis fille d'un lac
Qui ne s'est pas terni
D'un ciel limpide et bleu
Jusqu'à mes pieds tranquilles

Et fille d'un printemps
Qui ne finit jamais
Je ris des viols absurdes
Je suis toujours en fleur.

II

Pour tenir comme il se doit
Son rôle dans les ténèbres
Il se noue à la prison
Il en reflète les murs

Sa cruche est de chair immonde
Sa faim ressemble à son pain
Nul espoir ne le distrait
Et la porte joue pour rien

From Solitude to Solitude Towards Life

*In those days, an extraordinary resignation had suc-
ceeded terror and revolt. Holy women and martyrs swarmed.*

I

I am gentle with the strong
I am weak with the gentle
I know the words one must say
To inspire only forgetfulness

I am the daughter of a lake
Which has not dulled
Of a clear blue sky
Up to my peaceful feet

And daughter of spring
Which never ends
I laugh at senseless rapes
I am always in bloom.

II

To keep his role in the shadows
As it should be
He knots himself to the prison
He reflects its walls

His pitcher is of foul meat
His hunger resembles his bread
No hope distracts him
And the door plays to no end

Volute de sang de feu
Toute couverte d'épines
L'air qu'il respire déchire
Sa nudité intérieure

Demain de son coeur rouillé
Les vers même s'en iront
La place sera déserte
Dans un éternel désert.

III

Né de la sainte et du martyr
Voici pourtant l'enfant parfait
Au sommet d'une aurore intime

Léger et lourd comme un enfant
Il met au monde la confiance
Autant de soleils que de nuits

Il a ses mains dans les ruisseaux
Sa bouche danse en embrassant
Et ses yeux sont des chiens fidèles

Au crépuscule il est petit
Rêve et sommeil le dissimulent
Amour le fait grandir et jourir.

décembre 1945.

Wreath of blood of fire
Covered with thorns
The air he breathes tears
His inner nudity

Tomorrow even the worms will go
From his blighted heart
The place will be deserted
In an eternal desert.

III

Born of the saint and the martyr
Yet here is the perfect child
At the peak of intimate dawn

Light and heavy like a child
He gives birth to confidence
As many suns as nights

He has his hands in the streams
His mouth dances kissing
And his eyes are faithful hounds

At dusk he is little
Dream and sleep dissolve him
Love makes him grow and have pleasure.

Du fond de l'abîme

I

La lumière et la chaleur
Piétinées dispersées

Le pain
Volé aux naïfs

Le fil de lait
Lancé aux bêtes enragées

Quelques profondes mares de sang
Quelques incendies pétulants
Pour égayer ceux qui vont vivre
Vivre vivre sur leur fumier.

II

Au milieu du délire
Gorges tumultueuses et ventres dévorants
La morsure est soleil et lune le crachat
La blessure un écrin la souillure une perle
Tiède le sein pourri
La légende pourrie du sein maternel

Rose et verte la langue
La belle histoire de la langue changée en fée.

From the Depths of the Abyss

I

Light and warmth
Trodden dispersed

Bread
Stolen from the simple

The thread of milk
Hurled at raging beasts

A few deep pools of blood
A few lively burnings
To amuse those who are going to live
Live live on their dunghill.

II

At the pitch of madness
Tumultuous breasts and devouring wombs
The bite is sun and moon the spit
The wound a jewelcase the stain a pearl
The rotted breast is lukewarm
Rotted legend of the maternal breast

The tongue pink and green
Pretty story of the tongue changed into fay.

III

Ils n'étaient pas fous les mélancoliques
Ils étaient conquis digérés exclus
Par la masse opaque
Des monstres pratiques

Avaient leur âge de raison les mélancoliques
L'âge de la vie

Ils n'étaient pas là au commencement
A la création
Ils n'y croyaient pas
Et n'ont pas su du premier coup
Conjuguer la vie et le temps

Le temps leur paraissait long
La vie leur paraissait courte

Et des couvertures tachées par l'hiver
Sur des coeurs sans corps sur des coeurs sans nom
Faisaient un tapis de dégoût glacé
Même en plein été.

IV

Le solitaire toujours premier
Comme un ver dans une noix
Réapparaît le long des sinuosités
De la plus fraîche des cervelles
Le solitaire apprend à marcher de côté
A s'arrêter quand il est ivre de solitude
Le solitaire tourne ses pieds dans tous les sens
Il vague il rompt esquive feint

III

They were not mad the melancholics
They were conquered digested excluded
By the denseness
Of practical monsters

They had their age of reason the melancholics
The age of life

They were not there at the beginning
At creation
They did not believe in it
And did not know from the first shot
To conjugate life and time

Time seemed long to them
Life seemed short

And the blankets stained with winter
On hearts with no bodies on nameless hearts
Made a carpet of icy disgust
Even in mid-summer.

IV

The solitary always first
Like a worm in a nut
Reappears along the folds
Of the freshest of brains
The solitary learns to walk sideways
To stop when he is drunk with solitude
The solitary turns his steps in all the senses
He wanders he breaks dodges feigns

Il bouge mais bientôt
Tout bouge et lui fait peur
Le solitaire quand on l'appelle
Petit petit petit petit
Fait celui qui n'entend pas

En pleine viande fraîche
Comme un couteau rouillé
Le solitaire s'éternise
Et l'odeur du cadavre monte et s'éternise
Le miel de la force est farci d'ordures.

V

Je parle du fond de l'abîme
Et je vois le fond de l'abîme
L'homme creusé comme une mine
Comme un port sans vaisseaux
Comme un foyer sans feu

Pauvre visage sacrifié
Pauvre visage sans limites
Composé de tous les visages saccagés
Tu rêvais de balcons de voiles de voyages
Tu rêvais de printemps de baisers de bonté
Tu savais bien quels sont les droits et les devoirs
De la beauté mon beau visage dispersé

Il faudrait pour cacher ton horreur et ta honte
Des mains nouvelles des mains entières dans leur tâche
Mains travailleuses au présent
Et courageuses même en rêve.

He stirs but soon
Everything stirs and scares him
The solitary when called
Tiny tiny tiny tiny
Pretends to be deaf

In plump fresh meat
Like a rusty knife
The solitary drags on
And the odor of the corpse rises and drags on
The honey of force is stuffed with filth.

V

I speak from the depths of the abyss
And I see the depths of the abyss
Man hollowed out like a mine
Like a port without ships
Like a hearth without fire

Poor sacrificed face
Poor face without limits
Composed of all the ravaged faces
You dreamed of balconies of sails of voyages
You dreamed of spring of kisses of kindness
You knew well the rights and the tasks
Of beauty my handsome dispersed face

You need new hands to hide your horror and your shame
Hands whole in their task
Hands laboring in the present
And courageous even in dream.

VI

Je parle du fond de l'abîme
Je parle du fond de mon gouffre
C'est le soir et les ombres fuient
Le soir m'a rendu sage et fraternel
Il ouvre partout ses portes lugubres
Je n'ai pas peur j'entre partout
Je vois de mieux en mieux la forme humaine
Sans visage encore et pourtant
Dans un coin sombre où le mur est en ruines
Des yeux sont là aussi clairs que les miens
Ai-je grandi ai-je un peu de pouvoir.

VII

Nous sommes à nous deux la première nuée
Dans l'étendue absurde du bonheur cruel
Nous sommes la fraîcheur future
La première nuit de repos
Qui s'ouvrira sur un visage et sur des yeux nouveaux et purs
Nul ne pourra les ignorer.

VI

I speak from the depths of the abyss
I speak from the depths of my chasm
It is evening and shadows flee
Night made me wise and fraternal
It opens everywhere its gloomy doors
I am not afraid I enter everywhere
I see more and more clearly the human shape
Without features and yet
In a dark corner where the wall is in ruins
There are eyes as clear as mine
Have I grown have I a little power.

VII

We two are the first cloud
On the absurd plain of cruel happiness
We are the future freshness
The first night of repose
Which will open on a face and on eyes new and pure
No one may ignore them.

Grandeur d'hier et d'aujourd'hui

I

Les vagues des murs et l'air absent des enfants
Le plâtre gris des maisons mortes
La pierre morte autour des portes inutiles
Des enfants réduits et les murs leur vont bien
Comme à l'éclat de l'eau la boue du printemps
Comme à la beauté vierge une grimace bête

Et l'envie de vomir roule et rêve dans l'herbe.

II

Deux ombres sur la terre borgne
La mauvaise parole
Et la mauvaise nuit

Et la cloche de chair sous le linge fuyant
De la peur accroupie

Deux ombres sur la terre froide
Où les vers s'échauffent
Mieux que le blé

Sur la terre froide où parler descend
Où la femme est la fin de l'homme

Deux ombres une seule nuit
Définitive les coquins
Avaient raison de raisonner

Vitres salies feu confiné
Vitres brisées feu dispersé
Misère dépouillée d'espoir.

Grandeur of Yesterday and Today

I

Waves of walls and the absent air of children
Grey plaster of dead houses
Dead stones around useless doors
Children begging and the walls fit them
As the mud of spring suits the sparkle of water
As an idiotic grimace suits virgin beauty

And the desire to vomit wheels and dreams in the grass.

II

Two shadows on the one-eyed earth
The evil word
And the evil night

And the bell of flesh under the fleeing linen
Of crouched fear

Two shadows on the cold earth
Where worms warm themselves
Better than wheat

On the cold earth where speaking descends
Where woman is the end of man

Two shadows only one night
Definitive the scoundrels
Were right to reason

Dirtied windows imprisoned fire
Broken windows dispersed fire
Misery despoiled of hope.

III

Rien de plus pauvre qu'un enfant
Rien de plus pauvre que sa mère
Rien de plus pauvre qu'un soldat
Qu'un chien qu'un employé de banque

Ô confusion la terre borgne
Un oeil crevé pour ne rien voir
Un oeil au ciel pour oublier
L'hiver tue au hasard partout comme un avare

Son coeur s'éteint il est trop tard
Pour exalter sa vie passée
Et sa naissance dans les caves
Son âge d'or sous des haillons et sous des rides
Sous des soucis de marque sous son propre poids.

IV

Mais soudain de parler je me sens conquérant
Et plus clair et plus vif et plus fier et meilleur
Et plus près du soleil et plus sûr de durer
Un enfant naît en moi qui n'est pas d'aujourd'hui

Un enfant de toujours par un baiser unique
Plus insouciant qu'un premier papillon
A l'aube le printemps lui donne une seconde
Et la mort est vaincue un enfant sort des ruines

Derrière lui les ruines et la nuit s'effacent.

III

Nothing poorer than a child
Nothing poorer than his mother
Nothing poorer than a soldier
Than a dog than a bank employee

O confusion the one-eyed earth
One eye burst in order to see nothing
One eye to heaven to forget
Winter kills at random everywhere like a miser

His heart goes out it is too late
To exalt his past life
And his birth in cellars
His age of gold beneath rags and beneath wrinkles
Beneath care of rank beneath his own weight.

IV

But suddenly through speaking I feel triumphant
And clearer and more lively and prouder and better
And nearer the sun and more sure of enduring
A child is born in me who is not of today

A child of always from a unique kiss
Less troubled than a first butterfly
At dawn spring gives him a second
And death is conquered a child emerges from the ruins

Behind him the ruins and night fade away.

Puisqu'il n'est plus question de force

Tout est brisé par la parole la plus faible
Ombre d'idée idée de l'ombre mort heureuse
Le feu devient eau tiède et le pain est en miettes
Le sang farde un sourire et la foudre une larme
Le plomb caché par l'or pèse sur nos victoires
Nous n'avons rien semé qui ne soit ravagé
Par le bec minutieux des délices intimes
Les ailes rentrent dans l'oiseau pour le fixer.

Since It Is No Longer a Question of Force

Everything is broken by the weakest word
Shadow of idea idea of shadow happy death
Fire becomes tepid water and bread crumbles
Blood disguises a smile and thunder a tear
Lead hidden by gold weighs on our victories
We have sown nothing which has not been ravaged
By the precise beak of intimate delights
The wings return into the bird to nail him.

Ici

Une rue abandonnée
Une rue profonde et nue
Où les fous ont moins de peine
Que les sages à pourvoir
Aux jours sans pain sans charbon

C'est une question de taille
Tant de sages pour un fou
Mais rien par-delà l'immense
Majorité du bon sens
Un jour cru sans proportions

La rue comme une blessure
Qui ne se fermera pas
Le dimanche l'élargit
Le ciel est un ciel d'ailleurs
Roi d'un pays étranger

Un ciel rosé un ciel heureux
Respirant beauté santé
Sur la rue sans avenir
Qui coupe mon coeur en deux
Qui me prive de moi-même

Dans la rue de rien personne.

Here

A deserted street
A deep naked street
Where madmen have less trouble
Than the wise to provide
For the days without bread without coal

It is a matter of degree
So many sages for one fool
But nothing surpasses the immense
Majority of good sense
A raw day without proportions

The street like a wound
That will not close
Sunday makes it wider
The sky is a sky of elsewhere
King of a foreign country

A pink sky a happy sky
Breathing beauty health
On the street without future
Which cuts my heart in two
Which keeps me from myself

On the street of nothing, no one.

Saisons

I

Le centre du monde est partout et chez nous

Une rue s'offrit au soleil
Où était-elle et de quel poids
Dans la lumière suppliante
De l'hiver né du moindre amour

De l'hiver un enfant de rien
Avec sa suite de guenilles
Avec son cortège de peurs
Et de pieds froids sur des tombeaux

Dans le doux désert de la rue.

II

Le centre du monde est partout et chez nous

Soudain la terre bienvenue
Fut une rosé de fortune
Visible avec de blonds miroirs
Où tout chantait à rosé ouverte

A verte feuille et blanc métal
Poisseux d'ivresse et de chaleur
Or oui de l'or pour naître au sol
Sous l'écrasante multitude

Sous la vie accablante et bonne.

Seasons

I

The center of the world is everywhere and with us

A street gave itself to the sun
Where was it and what weight
In the pleading light
Of winter born of least love

Of winter a child of nothing
With its retinue of rags
With its cortege of fears
And of cold feet on tombs

In the gentle desert of the street.

II

The center of the world is everywhere and with us

Suddenly the welcome earth
Was a rose of luck
Visible with fair mirrors
Where everything sang to opened rose

To green leaf and white metal
Sticky with drunkenness and warmth
Gold yes gold to be born to the ground
Beneath the crushing multitude

Beneath life overpowering and good.

Notre mouvement

Nous vivons dans l'oubli de nos métamorphoses
Le jour est paresseux mais la nuit est active
Un bol d'air à midi la nuit le filtre et l'use
La nuit ne laisse pas de poussière sur nous

Mais cet écho qui roule tout le long du jour
Cet écho hors du temps d'angoisse ou de caresses
Cet enchaînement brut des mondes insipides
Et des mondes sensibles son soleil est double

Sommes-nous près ou loin de notre conscience
Où sont nos bornes nos racines notre but

Le long plaisir pourtant de nos métamorphoses
Squelettes s'animant dans les murs pourrissants
Les rendez-vous donnés aux formes insensées
A la chair ingénieuse aux aveugles voyants

Les rendez-vous donnés par la face au profil
Par la souffrance à la santé par la lumière
A la forêt par la montagne à la vallée
Par la mine à la fleur par la perle au soleil

Nous sommes corps à corps nous sommes terre à terre
Nous naissons de partout nous sommes sans limites.

Our Movement

We live in the oblivion of our changes
Day is lazy but night is active
A bowl of air at noon night filters and exhausts it
Night leaves no dust on us

But this echo which rolls all the day long
This echo outside of time of anguish or of caresses
This brutal chaining of insipid worlds
And of sensitive worlds its sun is double

Are we near or far from our consciousness
Where are our boundaries our roots our goal

Yet the long pleasure of our metamorphoses
Skeletons reviving in rotting walls
Rendezvous given to insensate forms
To the clever flesh to seeing blindmen

Rendezvous given by the front to the profile
By suffering to health by light
To the forest by the mountain to the valley
By the mine to the flower by the pearl to the sun

We are body to body we are earth to earth
We are born of everywhere we are without limits.

II.
Le temps déborde

*À J. et A. derniers reflets de mes amours, qui ont
tout fait pour dissiper la nuit qui m'envahit.*

II.
[Time Overflows]

To J. and A. last reflections of my loves, who have done everything to dissipate the night that invades me.

Je vis toujours

Et je me suis assis sans pudeur sur la vague
De ce fleuve lointain gaufré de soleil vert
Les arbres célébraient la nuit et les étoiles

J'ai vu clair dans la nuit toute nue
Dans la nuit toute nue quelle femme
M'a montré son visage s'est montrée toute nue
Sa beauté adulte était plus sérieuse
Que les lois sans pitié de la nécessité

Contre elle les toilettes de nature
Puériles exerçaient leurs armes éternelles
De fer et de marbre et de sel
Contre elle le diamant du ciel
S'émoussait et se ternissait

Pourtant c'était une beauté
De sable et de mousse et de crépuscule
Mais c'était une beauté
De chair de langue et de prunelles
Une beauté bourgeon et déchet des saisons

Beauté qui s'éteignait sous de vagues recontres
J'ai séparé des amoureux plus laids ensemble
Que séparés
Pour les sauver j'ai fait chanter la solitude
J'ai brisé leurs lèvres au carré

J'ai fait sécher j'ai eu le temps de faire sécher
Les fleurs sans remords d'un mensonge
Le fumier tout frais qui pleurait
Et les aubes mal réveillées

I Am Still Alive

And I sat down without shame on the wave
Of this distant river embossed with green sun
The trees celebrated the night and stars

I saw clearly in the stark naked night
In the stark naked night what woman
Showed me her face showed herself stark naked
Her adult beauty was more serious
Than the pitiless laws of necessity

Against her the costumes of nature
Childish tried their eternal arms
Of steel and marble and salt
Against her the diamond of the sky
Blunted and dulled

However she was a beauty
Of sand and moss and twilight
But she was a beauty
Of flesh of tongue and of pupils
A beauty bud and discard of the seasons

Beauty who grew dim with vague encounters
I separated lovers uglier together
Than apart
To save them I made solitude sing
I broke their lips squarely

I dried I had time to dry
The flowers without remorse of a lie
The dunghill all fresh that cried
And ill-awakened dawns

Mais j'ai fait rire les comédiens les plus amers
Épris de nudité et trop bien habillés
Ceux qui parlent à côté leurs yeux brûlent sans chaleur
Ceux qui parlent sciemment pour vieillir commodément
Les constructeurs de leur prison huilée bien cheminée
Porteurs de chaînes mains à menottes têtes à cornettes

Les globules bleus d'un monde décoloré
Sur le toit leurs rêves étaient à la cave
Ils ne cultivaient que l'éternité
Mon coeur et mon oeil
Sous l'espace intact tout était gelé

D'où êtes-vous sortie image sans azur
Spectatrice en vue
Sinon de moi qui dors si mal sur un grabat
D'où êtes-vous sortie touchant la terre de si près
Que je suis votre pas sur le pavé des rues

Où je m'ennuie si souvent où je me perdrai
Malgré tous les repères que j'ai posés lucide
Quand j'étais jeune et prévoyant
Quand l'ombre m'habitait
Quand je ne m'abreuvais que de vin transparent

Vous tout entière réglée par cette chair
Qui est la mienne au flanc du vide
Tremblante seulement
A l'idée d'échapper au monde indispensable
Vous précaire en dépit de mon espoir de vivre

But I made the most bitter comedians laugh
Infatuated with nudity and too well-dressed
Those who speak sideways their eyes burn without warmth
Those who speak knowingly to grow old with convenience
Builders of their oiled well-heated prison
Bearers of chains hands made for shackles heads made for coifs

The blue globules of a discolored world
On the roof their dreams were in the cellar
They cultivated only eternity
My heart and my eye
Beneath intact space everything was frozen

Where did you spring from image without azure
Woman watching in view
If not from me who sleeps so badly on a pallet
Where did you spring from touching so close to earth
That I am your step on the streets' pavement

Where I am bored so often that I will lose my way
In spite of all the landmarks that I lucidly posted
When I was young and cautious
When the shadows inhabited me
When I guzzled only transparent wine

You completely ruled by this flesh
Which is mine at the flank of emptiness
Trembling only
At the idea of escaping from the indispensable world
You precarious in spite of my hope to live

Il n'y a pas de dérision
Il n'y a rien qui soit faussé
Sinon ce qui n'est pas l'image sans midi
Qui s'impose la nuit sur la moelle
De ce fleuve où je me suis assis

Je vis encore et je partage
Le blé le pain de la beauté
Sans autre lumière que naître et qu'exister
Vous très basse et très haute dans la nudité
Du nord et du sud en un seul instant

La treille humaine est entre nous
Notre naissance de la femme est évidente
Et voici l'herbe qui poussa dans notre enfance

Es-tu malade ou fatigué
Es-tu dément ou simplement
Plus malheureux que d'habitude
Je n'ai pas envie de répondre

Car je crains trop en répondant
D'avoir le sort de ces joueurs
Qui jouent pour rien sur le velours
De leurs désirs de leurs douleurs

J'ai déniché les oeufs utiles
A ma faim pour ne past mourir
Mais au-delà j'oublie mes rêves
Au-delà je m'en veux à mort.

Octobre 1946.

There is no mockery
Nothing has been warped
Save that which is not the image without noon
Which obtrudes at night on the marrow
Of this river where I sit

I still live and share
The wheat the bread of beauty
Without other light than to be born and exist
You very low and very high in nudity
Of the north and south at one moment

The human trellis between us
Our birth from woman evident
And here is the grass which grew in our childhood

Are you ill or fatigued
Are you mad or simply
More unhappy than usual
I do not wish to reply

Because I am too afraid in answering
To have the luck of gamblers
Who play for nothing on the velvet
Of their desires of their woes

I have unearthed eggs useful
To my hunger in order not to die
But beyond I forget my dreams
Beyond I vex myself to death.

La puissance de l'espoir

Autant parler pour avouer mon sort:
Je n'ai rien mien, on m'a dépossédé
Et les chemins où je finirai mort
Je les parcours en esclave courbé;
Seule ma peine est ma propriété:
Larmes, sueurs et le plus dur effort.
Je ne suis plus qu'un objet de pitié
Sinon de honte aux yeux d'un monde fort.

J'ai de manger et de boire l'envie
Autant qu'un autre à en perdre la tête;
J'ai de dormir l'ardente nostalgie:
Dans la chaleur, sans fin, comme une bête.
Je dors trop peu, ne fais jamais la fête,
Jamais ne baise une femme jolie;
Pourtant mon coeur, vide, point ne s'arrête,
Malgré douleur mon coeur point ne dévie.

J'aurais pu rire, ivre de mon caprice.
L'aurore en moi pouvait creuser son nid
Et rayonner, subtile et protectrice,
Sur mes semblables qui auraient fleuri.
N'ayez pitié, si vous avez choisi
D'être bornés et d'être sans justice:
Un jour viendra où je serai parmi
Les constructeurs d'un vivant édifice,

La foule immense où l'homme est un ami.

3 novembre 1946.

The Power of Hope

I may as well speak to admit my lot:
I have nothing of my own, I was dispossessed
And the paths where I will end up dead
I travel them as a bent slave;
Only my pain is my property:
Tears, sweat and the hardest effort.
I am no more than an object of pity
If not of shame in the eyes of a strong world.

I have a mad longing to eat and drink
As much as anyone else;
I have an ardent nostalgia to sleep:
In the warmth, endlessly, like a beast.
I sleep too little, never celebrate,
Never make love to a pretty woman,
However, my heart, empty, does not stop,
In spite of misery my heart does not swerve.

I could have laughed, drunk with my caprice.
The dawn in me could have hollowed out its nest
And radiated, subtle and protective,
On my fellows who would have flourished.
Do not have pity, if you have chosen
To be limited and without justice:
A day will come when I will be among
The builders of a living edifice,

The immense crowd where man is a friend.

Un vivant parle pour les morts

Doux avenir, cet oeil crevé c'est moi,
Ce ventre ouvert et ces nerfs en lambeaux
C'est moi, sujet des vers et des corbeaux,
Fils du néant comme on est fils de roi.

J'aurai bientôt perdu mon apparence:
Je suis en terre au lieu d'être sur terre,
Mon coeur gâché vole avec la poussière,
Je n'ai de sens que par complète absence.

23 novembre 1946.

A Living Person Speaks for the Dead

Sweet future, I am this gouged eye,
This open stomach and these nerves in shreds
It's me, subject of worms and crows,
Son of nothingness as one is son of a king.

I will soon have lost my appearance:
I am in the earth instead of on earth,
My ruined heart flies with the dust,
I have sense only in complete absence.

L'extase

Je suis devant ce paysage féminin
Comme un enfant devant le feu
Souriant vaguement et les larmes aux yeux
Devant ce paysage où tout remue en moi
Où des miroirs s'embuent où des miroirs s'éclairent
Reflétant deux corps nus saison contre saison

J'ai tant de raisons de me perdre
Sur cette terre sans chemins et sous ce ciel sans horizon
Belles raisons que j'ignorais hier
Et que je n'oublierai jamais
Belles clés des regards clés filles d'elles-mêmes
Devant ce paysage où la nature est mienne

Devant le feu le premier feu
Bonne raison maîtresse
Étoile identifiée
Et sur la terre et sous le ciel hors de mon coeur et dans mon coeur
Second bourgeon première feuille verte
Que la mer couvre de ses ailes
Et le soleil au bout de tout venant de nous

Je suis devant ce paysage féminin
Comme une branche dans le feu.

24 novembre 1946.

Ecstasy

I face this feminine landscape
Like a child before the fire
Smiling vaguely and tears in my eyes
Before this landscape where everything moves in me
Where the mirrors cloud up where the mirrors clear
Reflecting two naked bodies season against season

I have so many reasons to lose myself
On this earth without paths and under this sky without horizon
Fine reasons that I did not know yesterday
And that I will never forget
Lovely keys of glances keys born of themselves
Before this landscape where nature is mine

Before the fire the first fire
Good prevailing reason
Identified star
And on earth and beneath the sky beyond my heart and in my heart
Second bud first green leaf
Which the sea covers with its wings
And the sun at the end of everything coming from us

I face this feminine landscape
Like a branch in the fire.

En vertu de l'amour

J'ai dénoué la chambre où je dors, où je rêve,
Dénoué la campagne et la ville où je passe,
Où je rêve éveillé, ou le soleil se lève,
Où, dans mes yeux absents, la lumière s'amasse.

Monde au petit bonheur, sans surface et sans fond,
Aux charmes oubliés sitôt que reconnus,
La naissance et la mort mêlent leur contagion
Dans les plis de la terre et du ciel confondus.

Je n'ai rien séparé mais j'ai doublé mon coeur.
D'aimer, j'ai tout crée: réel, imaginaire.
J'ai donné sa raison, sa forme, sa chaleur
Et son rôle immortel à celle qui m'éclaire.

27 novembre 1946.

Vingt-huit novembre mil neuf cent quarante-six

Nous ne vieillirons pas ensemble
                    Voici le jour
                          En trop: le temps déborde.
Mon amour si léger prend le poids d'un supplice.

By Virtue of Love

I have untied the room where I sleep, where I dream,
Untied the countryside and the city where I pass by,
Where I dream awakened, where the sun rises,
Where, in my absent eyes, light amasses.

Haphazard world, with no surface and bottomless,
Of charms forgotten as soon as taken in,
Birth and death blend their contagion
In the folds of the commingled earth and sky.

I have separated nothing but I have doubled my heart.
From loving, I have created all: real, imaginary.
I have given her reason, her form, her warmth
And her immortal role to the one who enlightens me.

November twenty-eighth nineteen forty-six

We will not grow old together
                    Here is the day
                            In excess: time overflows.
My love so light takes on the weight of torture.

Les limites du malheur

Mes yeux soudain horriblement
Ne voient pas plus loin que moi
Je fais des gestes dans le vide
Je suis comme un aveugle-né
De son unique nuit témoin

La vie soundain horriblement
N'est plus à la mesure du temps
Mon désert contredit l'espace
Désert pourri désert livide
De ma morte que j'envie

J'ai dans mon corps vivant les ruines de l'amour
Ma morte dans sa robe au col taché de sang.

The Limits of Grief

My eyes suddenly horribly
See no further than myself
I make gestures in the void
I am like the blind-born
Witness to his sole night

Life suddenly horribly
No longer measures up to time
My desert contradicts space
Rotted desert livid desert
Of my dead one whom I envy

I have in my living body the ruins of love
My dead one in her dress collar stained with blood.

Ma morte vivante

Dans mon chagrin rien n'est en mouvement
J'attends personne ne viendra
Ni de jour ni de nuit
Ni jamais plus de ce qui fut moi-même

Mes yeux se sont séparés de tes yeux
Ils perdent leur confiance ils perdent leur lumière
Ma bouche s'est séparée de ta bouche
Ma bouche s'est séparée du plaisir
Et du sens de l'amour et du sens de la vie
Mes mains se sont séparées de tes mains
Mes mains laissent tout échapper
Mes pieds se sont séparés de tes pieds
Ils n'avanceront plus il n'y a plus de routes
Ils ne connaîtront plus mon poids ni le repos

Il m'est donné de voir ma vie finir
Avec la tienne
Ma vie en ton pouvoir
Que j'ai crue infinie

Et l'avenir mon seul espoir c'est mon tombeau
Pareil au tien cerné d'un monde indifférent

J'étais si près de toi que j'ai froid près des autres.

My Living Dead

In my grief nothing is in movement
I wait no one will come
Neither by day nor by night
Nor ever again by that which I was

My eyes tore themselves from your eyes
They lose their confidence they lose their light
My mouth tore itself from your mouth
My mouth tore itself from pleasure
And from the sense of love and the sense of life
My hands tore themselves from your hands
My hands let everything drop
My feet tore themselves from your feet
They will not advance there are no more roads
They will no longer recognize my weight nor rest
It is my fate to see my life end
With yours
My life which I believed infinite
In your power

And the future my only hope is my tomb
Like yours ringed by an indifferent world

I was so close to you that I am cold near others.

Négation de la poésie

J'ai pris de toi tout le souci tout le tourment
Que l'on peut prendre à travers tout à travers rien
Aurais-je pu ne pas t'aimer
O toi rien que la gentillesse
Comme une pêche après une autre pêche
Aussi fondantes que l'été

Tout le souci tout le tourment
De vivre encore et d'être absent
D'écrire ce poème

Au lieu du poème vivant
Que je n'écrirai pas
Puisque tu n'es pas là

Les plus ténus dessins du feu
Préparent l'incendie ultime
Les moindres miettes de pain
Suffisent aux mourants

J'ai connu la vertu vivante
J'ai connu le bien incarné
Je refuse ta mort mais j'accepte la mienne
Ton ombre qui s'étend sur moi
Je voudrais en faire un jardin

L'arc débandé nous sommes de la même nuit
Et je veux continuer ton immobilité
Et le discours inexistant
Qui commence avec toi qui finira en moi
Avec moi volontaire obstiné révolté
Amoureux comme toi des charmes de la terre.

Negation of Poetry

I took from you all the worry all the torment
That one can take through all through nothing
Could I have not loved you
O you nothing but gentleness
Like one peach after another peach
As melting as summer

All the worry all the torment
Of living still and being absent
Of writing this poem

Instead of the living poem
That I will not write
Because you are not here

The most subtle designs of fire
Prepare the ultimate burning
The least crumbs of bread
Suffice to the dying

I knew living virtue
I knew good incarnate
I refuse your death I accept mine
I would like to make a garden
Of your shadow that stretches over me

The bow slackened we are of the same night
And I wish to continue your immobility
And the non-existent dialogue
Which begins with you which will end in me
With me self-willed obstinate rebel
In love like you with the charms of earth.

Dorée

Les draps humides de novembre
M'ensevelissent pour toujours
Le temps me file entre les doigts
La terre tourne en mes orbites

Où en est ce léger sourire
Qui commença un jour de mai
Sinon sur la bouche des morts
Malgré la peine des vivants

Où est la lettre sans réponse
Et la poussière des paroles
Cette confiance dans la vie
Qui tout à coup devient silence

Je nie les larmes leur lumière
Mes yeux ne sont plus de ce monde
Je suis passée tout est passé
Je suis une ombre dans le noir

Je suis le germe du désordre.

Gilded

The humid shrouds of November
Bury me forever
Time slips between my fingers
The earth turns in my orbits

Where did the light smile go
Which began one May day
If not to the lips of the dead
In spite of the pain of the living

Where is the letter without answer
And the dust of words
This confidence in life
Which suddenly becomes silence

I deny tears their light
My eyes are no longer of this world
I am past all is past
I am a shadow in the dark

I am the seed of disorder.

Notre vie

Notre vie tu l'as faite elle est ensevelie
Aurore d'une ville un beau matin de mai
Sur laquelle la terre a refermé son poing
Aurore en moi dix-sept années toujours plus claires
Et la mort entre en moi comme dans un moulin

Notre vie disais-tu si contente de vivre
Et de donner la vie à ce que nous aimions
Mais la mort a rompu l'équilibre du temps
La mort qui vient la mort qui va la mort vécue
La mort visible boit et mange à mes dépens

Morte visible Nusch invisible et plus dure
Que la soif et la faim à mon corps épuisé
Masque de neige sur la terre et sous la terre
Source des larmes dans la nuit masque d'aveugle
Mon passé se dissout je fais place au silence

Our Life

Our life you made it is buried
Dawn of a city one beautiful morning in May
On which the earth shut its fist
Dawn in me seventeen years always clearer
And death enters into me at will

Our life you used to say so happy to live
And to give life to that which we loved
But death disturbed the equilibrium of time
Death which comes death which goes death lived
Visible death drinks and eats at my expense

Visible death Nusch invisible and tougher
Than thirst and hunger to my exhausted body
Mask of snow on earth and below earth
Source of tears in the night mask of a blind man
My past dissolves I make way for silence.

Vivante et morte séparée

Vivante et morte séparée j'ai trébuché
Sur une tombe sur un corps
Qui soulève à peine la terre
Sur un corps dont j'étais construit
Sur la bouche qui me parlait
Et sur les yeux pourris de toutes les vertus
Mes mains mes pieds étaient les siens
Et mes désirs et mon poème étaient les siens
J'ai trébuché sur sa gaîté sur sa bonté
Qui maintenant ont les rigueurs de son squelette
Mon amour est de plus en plus concret il est en terre
Et non ailleurs j'imagine son odeur
Mon amour mon petit ma couronne d'odeurs
Tu n'avais rien de rien à faire avec la mort
Ton crâne n'avait pas connu la nuit des temps
Mon éphémère écoute je suis là je t'accompagne
Je te parle notre langue elle est minime et va d'un coup
Du grand soleil au grand soleil et nous mourons d'être vivants
Ecoute ici c'est notre chien ici notre maison
Ici c'est notre lit ici ceux qui nous aiment
Tous les produits de notre coeur de notre sang
Et de nos sens et de nos rêves
Je n'oublie rien de ces oiseaux de grande espèce
Qui nous guident qui nous enlèvent
Et qui font des trous dans l'azur
Comme volcans en pleine terre
Ma fille mon garçon petite mère et petit père
Mon poème ce soir aurait pu te distraire
Avec les mots précis que tu es fière de comprendre

The Quick and the Dead Separated

The quick and the dead separated I stumbled
On a tomb on a body
Which barely lifts the earth
On a body of which I was constructed
On the mouth which spoke to me
And on the eyes rotten with all virtues
My hands my feet were hers
And my desires and my poems were hers
I stumbled on her gaiety on her kindness
Which now have the rigors of her skeleton
My love is more and more concrete it is buried
And not elsewhere I imagine its odor
My love my little one my crown of odors
You had nothing but nothing to do with death
Your skull had not known the night of time
My may-fly listen I am there I accompany you
I speak our language to you it is minimal and goes suddenly
From bright sun to bright sun and we die to be living
Listen here is our dog here our house
Here is our bed and here those who love us
All the products of our heart of our blood
And of our senses and of our dreams
I forget nothing of those birds of large species
Who guide us who carry us off
And who make holes in the blue
Like volcanoes in the middle of the earth
My daughter my boy my little mother and little father
This evening my poem might have distracted you
With precise words that you are proud to understand

Avec les arrêts brusques des péripéties
Et les zibelines vives de la coquetterie
Et l'abasourdissante écume de la mer
Et la réminiscence et l'oubli délétère
Mon corps vivant charmant ma raison ma déraison
Ma séduction ma solitude mon plaisir et ma souffrance
Ma modestie et mon orgueil ma perversion et mon mérite
Toute petite et délabrée parfaite et pure
Pareille à un verre d'eau qui sera toujours bu
Je ne dors pas je suis tombé j'ai trébuché sur ton absence
Je suis sans feu sans force près de toi
Je suis le dessous de la bête je m'accroche
A notre chute à notre ruine
Je suis au-dessous de tes restes
J'aspire à ton néant je voudrais voir mon front
Comme un caillou loin dans la terre
Comme un bateau fondu dans l'eau
Mon petit qui pourtant m'engendras en orage
Me convertis en homme et m'aimas comme un sage
Ma voix n'a pas d'écho j'ai honte de parler
Je souffre pour toujours de ton silence ô mon amour.

With the sudden stops of reversals
And lively sables of coquetry
And the flabbergasting foam of the sea
And reminiscence and noxious forgetfulness
My living body charming my reason my unreason
My seduction my solitude my pleasure and my suffering
My modesty and my pride my perversion and my merit
You so small and shattered perfect and pure
Similar to a glass of water that will forever be drunk
I do not sleep I fell I stumbled on your absence
I am without fire without strength near you
I am the underside of the animal I cling
To our fall to our ruin
I am beneath your remains
I aspire to your nothingness I would like to see my forehead
Like a stone far in the earth
Like a boat dissolved in water
My little one who nevertheless engendered me in a storm
Converted me into a man and loved me like a sage
My voice has no echo I am ashamed to speak
I suffer forever from your silence o my love.

Notre vie

Nous n'irons pas au but un par un mais par deux
Nous connaissant par deux nous nous connaîtrons tous
Nous nous aimerons tous et nos enfants riront
De la légende noire où pleure un solitaire.

Our Life

We will not reach the goal one by one but by two
Knowing ourselves by two we will all know each other
We will all love each other and our children will laugh
At the dark legend where a lonely one cries.

III.
Corps mémorable

Dédicace

Ah! mille flammes, un feu, la lumière,
Une ombre!
Le soleil me suit,

Jacqueline me prolonge.

III.
[Memorable Body]

Dedication

Ah! thousand flames, a fire, the light,
A shadow!
The sun follows me,

Jacqueline extends me.

Grain de sable de mon salut

A force d'être claire et de donner à boire
Comme on ouvre la main pour libérer une aile
A force d'être partagée et réunie
Comme une bouche qui s'amasse ou qui frissonne
Comme une langue de raison qui s'abandonne
Deux bras qui s'ouvrent qui se ferment
Faisant le jour faisant la nuit et rallumant
Un feu qui couve mille enfants perdus d'espoir
A force d'incarner la nature fidèle
Forte comme un fruit mûr faible comme une aurore
Débordant des saisons et recouvrant des hommes
A force d'être comme un pré qui hume l'eau
Qui donne à boire à son terrain de haute essence
Innocent attendant un pas balbutiant

Comme un travail et comme un jeu comme un calcul
Faux jusqu'à l'os comme un cadeau et comme un rapt
A force d'être si patiente et souple et droite
A force de mêler le blé de la lumière
Aux caresses des chairs de la terre à minuit
A midi sans savoir si la vie est valable
Tu m'as ouvert un jour de plus est-ce aujourd'hui
Est-ce demain Toujours est nul Jamais n'est pas
Et tu risques de vivre aux dépens de toi-même

Moins que moi qui descends d'une autre et du néant.

Grain of Sand of My Salvation

By being clear and by offering drink
As one opens his hand to release a wing
By being split and reunited
Like a mouth that accumulates and shivers
Like a tongue of reason that surrenders itself
Two arms which open which close
Creating day creating night and rekindling
A fire that incubates a thousand hopeless children
By embodying faithful nature
Strong like a ripe fruit weak like a dawn
Overflowing with seasons and covering over men
By being like a meadow that breathes in water
That offers drink to its terrain of high essence
Innocent awaiting a mumbling step

Like a task and like a game like a computation
False to the bone like a gift and like an abduction
By being so patient and supple and straight
By mixing the wheat of light
With the caresses of the bodies of earth at midnight
At noon without knowing if life is valid
You open for me one more day is it today
Is it tomorrow Always is null Never is not
And you risk living at the expense of yourself

Less than me who descends from another and from nothingness.

Portrait en trois tableaux

I

Tes mains pourraient cacher ton corps
Car tes mains sont d'abord pour toi
Cacher ton corps tu fermerais les yeux
Et si tu les ouvrais on n'y verrait plus rien

Et sur ton corps tes mains font un très court chemin
De ton rêve à toi-même elles sont tes maîtresses
Au double de la paume est un miroir profond
Qui sait ce que les doigts composent et défont.

II

Si tes mains sont pour toi tes seins sont pour les autres
Comme ta bouche où tout revient prendre du goût
La voile des tes seins se gonfle avec la vague
De ta bouche qui s'ouvre et joint tous les rivages

Bonté d'être ivre de fatigue quand rougit
Ton visage rigide et que tes mains se vident
O mon agile et la plus lente et la plus vive
Tes jambes et tes bras passent la chair compacte

D'aplomb et renversée tu partages tes forces
A tous tu donnes de la joie comme une aurore
Qui se répand au fond du coeur d'un jour d'été
Tu oublies ta naissance et brûles d'exister.

Portrait in Three Tableaux

I

Your hands could hide your body
Because your hands are at first for you
To hide your body you would close your eyes
And if you opened them one would see there nothing more

And on your body your hands make a very short path
From your dream to yourself they are your mistresses
In the crease of your palm is a deep mirror
Who knows what the fingers compose and undo.

II

If your hands are for you your breasts are for others
Like your mouth where everything returns to take on flavor
The sail of your breasts swells with the wave
Of your mouth which opens and joins all shores.

Kindness of being drunk with fatigue when
Your tense face flushes and your hands empty themselves
O my agile one and the slowest and the quickest
Your legs and your arms surpass the compact flesh

Upright and reversed you share your forces
To all you give joy like a dawn
Which spreads into the heart of a summer day
You forget your birth and burn to exist.

III

Et tu te fends comme un fruit mûr ô savoureuse
Mouvement bien en vue spectacle humide et lisse
Gouffre franchi très bas en volant lourdement
Je suis partout en toi partout où bat ton sang

Limite de tous les voyages tu résonnes
Comme un voyage sans nuages tu frissonnes
Comme une pierre dénudée aux feux d'eau folle
Et ta soif d'être nue éteint toutes les nuits.

Entre la lune et le soleil

Je te le dis gracieuse et lumineuse
Ta nudité lèche mes yeux d'enfant
Et c'est l'extase des chasseurs heureux
D'avoir fait croître un gibier transparent
Qui se dilate en un vase sans eau
Comme une graine à l'ombre d'un caillou

Je te vois nue arabesque nouée
Aiguille molle à chaque tour d'horloge
Soleil étale au long d'une journée
Rayons tressés nattes de mes plaisirs.

III

And you split like a ripe fruit o savory woman
Movement in full view spectacle humid and sleek
Chasm cleared very low by flying heavily
I am everywhere in you everywhere where your blood beats

Limit of all voyages you resonate
Like a voyage without clouds you shudder
Like a stone denuded at the fireworks of water
And your thirst to be naked extinguishes all nights.

Between the Moon and the Sun

I tell you gracious and luminous woman
Your nudity licks my childlike eyes
And it is the ecstasy of happy hunters
To have increased a transparent game
Which expands in a vase without water
Like a seed in a shadow of a stone

I see you nude knotted arabesque
Hand slack at each turn of the clock
Sun slow along the length of a day
Plaited rays braids of my pleasures.

D'un et de deux, de tous

Je suis le spectateur et l'acteur et l'auteur
Je suis la femme et son mari et leur enfant
Et le premier amour et le dernier amour
Et le passant furtif et l'amour confondu

Et de nouveau la femme et son lit et sa robe
Et ses bras partagés et le travail de l'homme
Et son plaisir en flèche et la houle femelle
Simple et double ma chair n'est jamais en exil

Car où commence un corps je prends forme et conscience
Et même quand un corps se défait dans la mort
Je gis en son creuset j'épouse son tourment
Son infamie honore et mon coeur et la vie.

Of One and Two, of Everyone

I am the spectator and actor and author
I am the wife and her husband and their child
And first love and last love
And the stealthy passerby and love confounded

And woman anew and her bed and her dress
And her arms shared and the labor of man
And his rise of pleasure and the female swell
Single and double my flesh is never in exile

For where a body begins I take shape and consciousness
And even when a body becomes undone in death
I lie in its crucible I marry its torment
Its infamy honors both my heart and life.

Puisqu'il le faut

Dans le lit plein ton corps se simplifie
Sexe liquide univers de liqueurs
Liant des flots qui sont autant de corps
Entiers complets de la nuque aux talons
Grappe sans peau grappe-mère en travail
Grappe servile et luisante de sang
Entre les seins les cuisses et les fesses
Régentant l'ombre et creusant le chaleur
Lèvre étendue à l'horizon du lit
Sans une éponge pour happer la nuit
Et sans sommeil pour imiter la mort.

———————

Frapper la femme monstre de sagesse
Captiver l'homme à force de patience
Doucer la femme pour éteindre l'homme
Tout contrefaire afin de tout réduire
Autant rêver d'être seul et aveugle.

———————

Je n'ai de coeur qu'en mon front douloureux.

———————

L'après-midi nous attendions l'orage
Il éclatait lorsque la nuit tombait
Et les abeilles saccageaient la ruche
Puis de nos mains tremblantes maladroites
Nous allumions par habitude un feu
La nuit tournant autour de sa prunelle
Et nous disions je t'aime pour y voir.

Since It Is a Must

In the full bed your body simplifies itself
Liquid sex universe of liqueurs
Tying waves which are as many bodies
Whole complete from nape to heels
Cluster without skin new wine fermenting
Cluster slavish and gleaming with blood
Between breasts thighs and buttocks
Governing the shadow and excavating warmth
Lip stretched out on the bed's horizon
Without a sponge to snap up night
And without sleep to imitate death.

––––––––––

To strike woman monster of wisdom
To captivate man through patience
To subdue woman to slake man
Feign everything in order to cheapen it all
Might as well dream of being alone and blind.

––––––––––

I only take heart in my sorrowful brow.

––––––––––

In the afternoon we would wait for the storm
It burst just as night was falling
And the bees pillaged the hive
Then with our trembling clumsy hands
We would light a fire out of habit
Night turned around the pupil of her eye
And we said I love you to see into it.

Le temps comblé la langue au tiers parfum
Se retenait au bord de chaque bouche
Comme un mourant au bord de son salut
Jouer jouir n'étaient plus enlacés
Du sol montait un corps bien terre à terre
L'ordre gagnait et la désir pesait
Branch maîtresse n'aimait plus le vent

Par la faute d'un corps sourd
Par la faute d'un corps mort
D'un corps injuste et dément.

Sans avenir

La femme cerne un petit homme coléreux
Qui ne veut pas dormir ni rêver mais connaître
Et qui refuse de mourir sans tout aimer

Petite femme patiente tu le calmes
Et tu l'affoles selon l'ordre de ta chair

Tu pèses sur son coeur tu allèges son corps
Dans le noir redoubtable tu l'immobilises
Il vit sans avenir.

Time filled the tongue to the third perfume
Held fast to the brim of each mouth
Like a dying person at the brink of his salvation
To play to take pleasure were no longer intertwined
From the soil arose a body very down to earth
Order prevailed and desire became heavy
The top limb no longer liked the wind

Through the fault of a deaf body
Through the fault of a dead body
Of a body unjust and insane.

Without Future

The woman encircles an irascible little man
Who does not wish to sleep or to dream but to know
And who refuses to die without loving everything

Little patient woman you calm him
And you madden him according to the order of your flesh

You weigh on his heart you unburden his body
In the formidable dark you immobilize him
He lives without future.

Répétitions
Tout près du sommeil exigeant

L'oeil à force d'espace et d'éclat délirants
L'oeil fait vivre et plus loin le plomb du corps s'écoule

La barque de la bouche est menée par la langue
Muette tout humide elle éclaire les flots

Les larges mains ne savent rien de leur pouvoir
Et leurs épis jonchent la peau de la moisson

Doigts des éclairs caresses d'or broderies fauves
Dans les paumes les seins et les fesses s'insurgent

De nuit entre les yeux de jour entre les jambes
C'est le même palais qui flambe en un instant

C'est un trésor absurde un flot de diamants
Qui provoque l'orage et déchire les reins

C'est la main ignorante et la langue accordée
Pour la première fois sous un ciel féminin

Et le milieu du corps définissant l'orage
Balance de raison pour peser notre vie

C'est toi c'est moi nous sommes doubles dans nos songes.

Rehearsals
Very Close to Exacting Sleep

The eye through delirious light and space
The eye gives life and further on the lead of the body flows

The barque of the mouth is steered by the tongue
Mute all moist it lights the waves

The wide hands know nothing of their power
And their ears of grain strew the skin of the harvest

Fingers of lightning caresses of gold wild embroideries
In the palms the breasts and buttocks rise to battle

At night between the eyes in daylight between the legs
It is the same palace which blazes in an instant

It is an absurd treasure a torrent of diamonds
Which provokes the storm and tears the loins

It is the ignorant hand and the tuned tongue
For the first time under a feminine sky

And the center of the body defining the storm
Scale of reason to weigh our life

It is you it is me we are doubles in our dreams.

Mais elle

Elle ne vit que par sa forme
Elle a la forme d'un rocher
Elle a la forme de la mer
Elle a les muscles du rameur
Tous les rivages la modèlent

Ses mains s'ouvrent sur une étoile
Et ses yeux cachent le soleil
Une eau lavée le feu brûlé
Calme profond calme créé
Incarnant l'aube et le couchant

Pour en avoir connu le fond
Je sers la forme de l'amour
Elle ce n'est jamais la même
Je sers des ventres et des fronts
Qui s'effacent et se transforment

Fraîche saison promesse chaude
Elle est à l'échelle des fleurs
Et des heures et des couleurs
Niveau de force et de faiblesse
Elle est ma perte de conscience

Mais je refuse son hiver.

But She

She lives only by her form
She has the form of a rock
She has the form of the sea
She has the muscles of a rower
All shores shape her

Her hands open on a star
And her eyes hide the sun
Cleansed water burned fire
Deep calm created calm
Embodying dawn and sunset

Because I have known its depths
I serve the form of love
It is never the same
I serve bellies and brows
Which fade and are transformed

Cool season warm promise
She is on the scale of flowers
And of hours and of colors
Level of force and of weakness
She is my loss of consciousness

But I refuse her winter.

Je t'ai imaginée

Le grand merci que je dois à la vie
Non à la mienne mais à toute vie
Car tu es femme entière à la folie
Et rien n'a pu te réduire à toi-même
Dors mon enfance ma confiance d'or
Sur la litière où nous n'avons qu'un coeur
Fuyez misères à visage d'homme
Veiller sur toi c'est rêver d'être toi

C'est être sérieux
Sans avoir rien appris
Si de raison ma tête s'éclairait
Je ne serais qu'un homme qui a tort
Baiser m'enivre un peu plus qu'il ne faut
Je suis futur et rien n'a de limites
Toi l'endormie moi l'homme sans sommeil
Nous partageons une marge indistincte
De fruits de fleurs de fruits couvrant les fleurs
Et de soleil s'enchevêtrant aux nuits

Comme si la nuit
Etait la terre des couleurs
Comme si la verdure et l'automne
Naissaient du gel fixé aux branches
Comme si ces vivants que l'on nomme
Sel de la terre ou lumière de nuit
Ne pouvaient pas se contrefaire

I Imagined You

The great favour that I owe to life
Not to mine but to all life
Because you are wholly extravagantly woman
And nothing has been able to reduce you to yourself
Sleep my childhood my golden confidence
On the litter where we have but one heart
Flee miseries with men's faces
To watch over you is to dream of being you

It is to be serious
Without having learned anything
If my head brightened with reason
I would only be a man who is wrong
Lovemaking intoxicates me a bit more than it should
I am future and nothing has limits
You the sleeping woman me the sleepless man
We share an indistinct border
Of fruits of flowers of fruits covering flowers
And of sun entangled with nights

As if night
Were the earth of colors
As if greenery and autumn
Were born from the frost glued to branches
As if these living that one names
Salt of the earth or light of night
Could not disguise themselves

Ne pas avoir un ventre déférent
Des seins décents aimables complaisants
Et ces mains obstinées au travail des caresses
Où en es-tu je vis j'ai vécu je vivrai
Je crée je t'ai créée je te transformerai

Pourtant je suis toujours par toi l'enfant sans ombre
Je t'ai imaginée.

Jeunesse engendre la jeunesse

J'ai été comme un enfant
Et comme un homme
J'ai conjugué passionnément
Le verbe être et ma jeunesse
Avec le désir d'être homme

On se veut quand on est jeune
Un petit homme
Je me voudrais un grand enfant
Plus fort et plus juste qu'un homme
Et plus lucide qu'un enfant

Jeunesse force fraternelle
Le sang répète le printemps
L'aurore apparaît à tout âge
A tout âge s'ouvre la porte
Etincelante du courage

Comme un dialogue d'amoureux
Le coeur n'a qu'une seule bouche.

Not have a submissive belly
Decent likable obliging breasts
And these hands obstinate at the work of caresses
Where are you I live I have lived I will live
I create I created you I will transform you

However I am always by you the child without shadow
I imagined you.

Youth Begets Youth

I was like a child
And like a man
I conjugated passionately
The verb to be and my youth
With the desire to be a man

When one is young one wants to be
A little man
I would like to be a grown child
Stronger and more just than a man
And more lucid than a child

Youth fraternal strength
Blood repeats spring
Dawn appears at every age
At every age the glittering
Door of courage opens

Like a lover's dialogue
The heart has only a single mouth.

Prête aux baisers résurrecteurs

Pauvre je ne peux pas vivre dans l'ignorance
Il me faut voir entendre et abuser
T'entendre nue et te voir nue
Pour abuser de tes caresses

Par bonheur ou par malheur
Je connais ton secret par coeur
Toutes les portes de ton empire
Celle des yeux celle des mains
Des seins et de ta bouche où chaque langue fond

Et la porte du temps ouverte entre tes jambes
La fleur des nuits d'été aux lèvres de la foudre
Au seuil du paysage où la fleur rit et pleure
Tout en gardant cette pâleur de perle morte
Tout en donnant ton coeur tout en ouvrant tes jambes

Tu es comme la mer tu berces les étoiles
Tu es le champ d'amour tu lies et tu sépares
Les amants et les fous
Tu es la faim le pain la soif l'ivresse haute

Et le dernier mariage entre rêve et vertu.

Ready for Resurrecting Kisses

Needy I cannot live in ignorance
I must see hear and overdo
Hear you naked and see you naked
To take advantage of your caresses

For better or for worse
I know your secret by heart
All the doors of your empire
That of the eyes that of the hands
Of the breasts and of your mouth where each tongue melts

And the door of time opens between your legs
The flower of summer nights at the lips of lightning
At the threshold of the landscape where the flower laughs and cries
While keeping this pallor of dead pearl
While giving your heart while opening your legs

You are like the sea you rock the stars
You are the field of love you bind and you separate
Lovers and madmen
You are hunger bread thirst drunkenness high

And the last marriage between dream and virtue.

A l'infini

Elle surgissait de ses ressemblances
Et de ses contraires

On la voyait mieux parfois plus publique
Que cachant ses seins sous un coeur de mère

Peut-elle inspirer de l'indifférence
Celle qui est moi-même

———————

Elle exalte mon frère
Mon frère la première image

Le soleil brille à travers lui il est né d'elle
Et c'est ainsi que je suis sûr que chacun l'aime

———————

Elle surgissait de l'homme
Et l'homme surgissait d'elle
Elle surgissait du désir de l'homme
D'un homme
De moi
Et d'un autre homme
Et peut-être aussi d'une femme
De plusieurs femmes désirables idéales
Et de plusieurs femmes sans charmes

To the Infinite

She sprang from her likenesses
And from her opposites

One saw her better at times more public
Than hiding her breasts beneath a mother's heart

Can she inspire indifference
She who is myself

———————

She exalts my brother
My brother the first image

The sun glistens through him it is born from her
And that's how I am sure that everyone loves him

———————

She sprang from man
And man arose from her
She sprang from the desire of man
Of one man
Of myself
And of another man
And perhaps also of a woman
Of many women desirable ideal
And from many women without charms

Surgissait des enfances vagues
Des plus beaux rêves en spirales colorées
Et des réalités rigides
Bossues cassées blanches et noires
Rêve et réalité la rosé et le rosier
La douleur et ses murs le long d'une rue calme
La douleur acceptable et le plaisir possible

Sèche
Des pieds à la tete
Elle allait sur les marais
Et s'enlisait dans les dunes

Moi frais ou chaud
De temps en temps j'étais son lit
Ses draps blancs ses draps sales
Et son plaisir intime

Son sang naviguait à la rame
Autour de l'île de son coeur
Nous chassions à deux le sommeil
Deux soleils se levaient en nous.

Arose from vague childhoods
From most beautiful dreams in tinted spirals
And from rigid realities
Broken hunchbacks white and black
Dream and reality the rose and the rosebush
Sorrow and its walls the length of a calm street
Acceptable sorrow and possible pleasure

———————

Dry
From head to toe
She went into the marshlands
And sank into the dunes

Myself cool or warm
From time to time I was her bed
Her white sheets her soiled sheets
And her intimate pleasure

Her blood rowed to the oar
Around the isle of her heart
Together we chased sleep
Two suns arose in us.

Une livre de chair

Je suis un homme dans le vide
Un sourd un aveugle un muet
Sur un immense socle de silence noir

Rien cet oubli sans bornes
Cet absolu d'un zéro répété
La solitude complétée

Le jour est sans tache et la nuit est pure

———————

Parfois je prends tes sandales
Et je marche vers toi

Parfois je revêts ta robe
Et j'ai tes seins et j'ai ton ventre

Alors je me vois sous ton masque
Et je me reconnais.

A Pound of Flesh

I am a man in the void
Deaf blind a mute
On an immense pedestal of black silence

Nothing this oblivion without bounds
This absolute of a repeated zero
Solitude completed

The day is stainless and the night is pure

———————

Sometimes I take your sandals
And I walk toward you

Sometimes I put on your dress
And I have your breasts and I have your womb

Then I see myself beneath your mask
And I recognize myself.

Je parle en rêve

Dans les veines de notre ville
S'allongeaient de bons diables d'hommes
Un chapelet d'amours d'enfants
Et sages comme des cristaux

Sur tous les chemins de nos yeux
S'étalaient des femmes sacrées
Comme des voiles de mariées
Intacts ou rapiécés onctueux et pesants

Je parle en rêve et je transmets
Le court moment du grand repos
Le temps où rien n'est impossible
La chair en plus le miel en trop

Sourire aux anges est réel.

I Speak in Dream

In the veins of our city
Stretched out beside jolly good fellows
A rosary of loves of children
Well-behaved like crystals

On all the paths of our eyes
Sacred women were spread out
Like the veils of brides
Intact or patched unctuous and heavy

I speak in dream and I transmit
The brief moment of the great rest
The time where nothing is impossible
The flesh added the honey in excess

To smile blissfully is real.

IV.
Le phénix

Le Phénix, c'est le couple—Adam et Eve—qui est et n'est pas le premier.

IV.
[The Phoenix]

The Phoenix is the couple—Adam and Eve—that is and is not the first.

Le phénix

Je suis le dernier sur ta route
Le dernier printemps la dernière neige
Le dernier combat pour ne pas mourir

Et nous voici plus bas et plus haut que jamais.

———————

Il y a de tout dans notre bûcher
Des pommes de pin des sarments
Mais aussi des fleurs plus fortes que l'eau

De la boue et de la rosée.

———————

La flamme est sous nos pieds la flamme nous couronne
A nos pieds des insectes des oiseaux des hommes
Vont s'envoler

Ceux qui volent vont se poser.

———————

Le ciel est clair la terre est sombre
Mais la fumée s'en va au ciel
Le ciel a perdu tous ses feux.

La flamme est restée sur la terre.

———————

La flamme est la nuée du coeur
Et toutes les branches du sang
Elle chante notre air

The Phoenix

I am the last on your path
The last spring the last snow
The last struggle not to die

And here we are lower and higher than ever.

———————

There is everything in our pyre
Fir-cones vine-shoots
But also flowers stronger than water

Mud and dew.

———————

The flame below our feet flame coronates us
At our feet insects birds men
Are going to fly away

Those who fly will alight.

———————

The sky is clear earth is dark
But smoke rises to the sky
The sky has lost all its flares

The flame remained on earth.

———————

The flame is the storm cloud of the heart
And all the branches of the blood
It sings our air

Elle dissipe la buée de notre hiver.

Nocturne et en horreur a flambé le chagrin
Les cendres ont fleuri en joie et en beauté
Nous tournons toujours le dos au couchant

Tout a la couleur de l'aurore.

It dissolves the vapor of our winter.

Nocturnal and in horror blazed sorrow
Ashes flowered in joy and beauty
We always turn our backs on the sunset

Everything has the color of dawn.

Dominique aujourd'hui présente

Toutes les choses au hasard
Tous les mots dits sans y penser
Et qui sont pris comme ils sont dits
Et nul n'y perd et nul n'y gagne

Les sentiments à la dérive
Et l'effort le plus quotidien
Le vague souvenir des songes
L'avenir en butte à demain

Les mots coincés dans un enfer
De roues usées de lignes mortes
Les choses grises et semblables
Les hommes tournant dans le vent

Muscles voyants squelette intime
Et la vapeur des sentiments
Le coeur réglé comme un cercueil
Les espoirs réduits à néant

Tu es venue l'après-midi crevait la terre
Et la terre et les hommes ont changé de sens
Et je me suis trouvé réglé comme un aimant
Réglé comme une vigne

A l'infini notre chemin le but des autres
Des abeilles volaient futures de leur miel
Et j'ai multiplié mes désirs de lumière
Pour en comprendre la raison

Dominique Present Today

All things at random
All words spoken without thinking
And which are taken as they are said
And no one loses and no one gains by it

Feelings adrift
And the most ordinary effort
The vague memory of dreams
The future exposed to tomorrow

Words wedged in a hell
Of used wheels of dead lines
Things grey and similar
Men turning in the wind

Gaudy muscles intimate skeleton
And the haze of emotions
The heart ruled like a coffin
Hopes reduced to nothingness

You arrived the afternoon split the earth
And the earth and men changed direction
And I found myself ruled like a compass
Ruled like a vineyard

To the infinite our path the goal of others
The bees flew futures pregnant with their honey
And I have multiplied my desires of light
To understand the reason for them

Tu es venue j'étais très triste j'ai dit oui
C'est à partir de toi que j'ai dit oui au monde
Petite fille je t'aimais comme un garçon
Ne peut aimer que son enfance

Avec la forcé d'un passé tres loin très pur
Avec le feu d'une chanson sans fausse note
La pierre intacte et le courant furtif du sang
Dans la gorge et les lèvres

Tu es venue le voeu de vivre avait un corps
Il creusait la nuit lourde il caressait les ombres
Pour dissoudre leur boue et fondre leurs glaçons
Comme un oeil qui voit clair

L'herbe fine figeait le vol des hirondelles
Et l'automne pesait dans le sac des ténèbres
Tu es venue les rives libéraient le fleuve
Pour le mener jusqu'à la mer

Tu es venue plus haute au fond de ma douleur
Que l'arbre séparé de la forêt sans air
Et le cri du chagrin du doute s'est brisé
Devant le jour de notre amour

Gloire l'ombre et la honte ont cédé au soleil
Le poids s'est allégé le fardeau s'est fait rire
Gloire le souterrain est devenu sommet
La misère s'est effacée

La place d'habitude où je m'abêtissais
Le couloir sans réveil l'impasse et la fatigue
Se sont mis à briller d'un feu battant des mains
L'éternité s'est dépliée

You arrived I was very sad I said yes
Starting with you I said yes to the world
Little girl I loved you as a boy
Can only love his childhood

With the strength of a past very distant very pure
With the fire of a song without false note
The stone intact and the furtive current of blood
In the throat and lips

You arrived the desire to live had a body
It hollowed the heavy night it caressed the shadows
To dissolve their mud and melt their ice drifts
Like an eye that sees clearly

The fine grass arrested the swallow's flight
And autumn was heavy in the sack of darkness
You arrived the shores released the river
To lead it down to the sea

You arrived at the bottom of my grief higher
Than the tree separated from the forest without air
And the cry of grief of doubt broke
Before the day of our love

Glory the shadow and shame gave way to the sun
The weight grew lighter the burden made itself laugh
Glory the underground became summit
Misery erased itself

The usual place where I made myself dumb
The corridor without awakening the impasse and fatigue
Began to shine with a fire clapping hands
Eternity unfolded

O toi mon agitée et ma calme pensée
Mon silence sonore et mon écho secret
Mon aveugle voyante et ma vue dépassée
Je n'ai plus eu que ta présence

Tu m'as couvert de ta confiance.

Air vif

J'ai regardé devant moi
Dans la foule je t'ai vue
Parmi les blés je t'ai vue
Sous un arbre je t'ai vue

Au bout de tous mes voyages
Au fond de tous mes tourments
Au tournant de tous les rires
Sortant de l'eau et du feu

L'été l'hiver je t'ai vue
Dans ma maison je t'ai vue
Entre mes bras je t'ai vue
Dans mes rêves je t'ai vue

Je ne te quitterai plus.

O you my restless one and my calm thought
My sonorous silence and my secret echo
My blind woman seer and my sight outstripped
I had nothing but your presence

You sheltered me with your trust.

Lively Air

I looked before me
In the crowd I saw you
In the wheatfields I saw you
Beneath a tree I saw you

At the end of all my travels
At the bottom of all my torments
At the turning point of all laughter
Springing from water and fire

Summer winter I saw you
In my house I saw you
In my arms I saw you
In my dreams I saw you

I will not leave you again.

Printemps

Il y a sur la plage quelques flaques d'eau
Il y a dans les bois des arbres fous d'oiseaux
La neige fond dans la montagne
Les branches des pommiers brillent de tant de fleurs
Que le pâle soleil recule

C'est par un soir d'hiver dans un monde très dur
Que je vis ce printemps près de toi l'innocente
Il n'y a pas de nuit pour nous
Rien de ce qui périt n'a de prise sur toi
Et tu ne veux pas avoir froid

Notre printemps est un printemps qui a raison.

Spring

There are some pools of water on the beach
There are trees mad with birds in the woods
Snow is melting in the mountain
The branches of the apple tree shine with so many flowers
That the pale sun withdraws

It is by a winter evening in a very harsh world
That I live this spring near you the innocent woman
There is no night for us
Nothing of that which perishes has a hold on you
And you do not want to be cold

Our spring is a spring which is right.

Je t'aime

Je t'aime pour toutes les femmes que je n'ai pas connues
Je t'aime pour tous les temps où je n'ai pas vécu
Pour l'odeur du grand large et l'odeur du pain chaud
Pour la neige qui fond pour les premières fleurs
Pour les animaux purs que l'homme n'effraie pas
Je t'aime pour aimer
Je t'aime pour toutes les femmes que je n'aime pas

Qui me reflète sinon toi-même je me vois si peu
Sans toi je ne vois rien qu'une étendue déserte
Entre autrefois et aujourd'hui
Il y a eu toutes ces morts que j'ai franchies sur de la paille
Je n'ai pas pu percer le mur de mon miroir
Il m'a fallu apprendre mot par mot la vie
Comme on oublie

Je t'aime pour ta sagesse qui n'est pas la mienne
Pour la santé
Je t'aime contre tout ce qui n'est qu'illusion
Pour ce coeur immortel que je ne détiens pas
Tu crois être le doute et tu n'es que raison
Tu es le grand soleil qui me monte à la tete
Quand je suis sûr de moi.

I Love You

I love you for all the women I have not known
I love you for all the time I have not lived
For the odor of the open sea and the odor of warm bread
For the snow which melts for the first flowers
For the pure animals man doesn't frighten
I love you to love
I love you for all the women I do not love

Who reflects me if not you I see myself so little
Without you I see nothing but an extended desert
Between long ago and today
There are all those deaths that I crossed on the straw
I have not been able to pierce the wall of my mirror
I have had to learn life word by word
As one forgets

I love you for your wisdom which is not mine
For health
I love you against everything that is but illusion
For the immortal heart that I do not possess
You believe you are doubt you are only reason
You are the great sun which makes me drunk
When I am sure of me.

Certitude

Si je te parle c'est pour mieux t'entendre
Si je t'entends je suis sûr de comprendre

Si tu souris c'est pour mieux m'envahir
Si tu souris je vois le monde entier

Si je t'étreins c'est pour me continuer
Si nous vivons tout sera à plaisir

Si je te quitte nous nous souviendrons
Et nous quittant nous nous retrouverons.

Certainty

If I speak it is to hear you better
If I hear you I am sure to understand

If you smile it is the better to invade me
If you smile I see the whole world

If I clasp you it is to extend myself
If we live everything will be wanton

If I leave you we will remember each other
And parting we will rediscover one another.

Nous deux

Nous deux nous tenant par la main
Nous nous croyons partout chez nous
Sous l'arbre doux sous le ciel noir
Sous tous les toits au coin du feu
Dans la rue vide en plein soleil
Dans les yeux vagues de la foule
Auprès des sages et des fous
Parmi les enfants et les grands
L'amour n'a rien de mystérieux
Nous sommes l'évidence même
Les amoureux se croient chez nous.

We Two

We two holding each other by the hand
We believe ourselves to be everywhere at home
Beneath the gentle tree beneath the black sky
Beneath all the roofs by the fireside
In the empty street in broad daylight
In the vague eyes of the crowd
Near sages and fools
Among children and grownups
There is nothing mysterious about love
We are the very proof
Lovers believe they are with us.

La mort l'amour la vie

J'ai cru pouvoir briser la profondeur l'immensité
Par mon chagrin tout nu sans contact sans écho
Je me suis étendu dans ma prison aux portes vierges
Comme un mort raisonnable qui a su mourir
Un mort non couronné sinon de son néant
Je me suis étendu sur les vagues absurdes
Du poison absorbé par amour de la cendre
La solitude m'a semblé plus vive que le sang

Je voulais désunir la vie
Je voulais partager la mort avec la mort
Rendre mon coeur au vide et le vide à la vie
Tout effacer qu'il n'y ait rien ni vitre ni buée
Ni rien devant ni rien derrière rien entier
J'avais éliminé le glaçon des mains jointes
J'avais éliminé l'hivernale ossature
Du voeu de vivre qui s'annule.

Tu es venue le feu s'est alors ranimé
L'ombre a cédé le froid d'en bas s'est étoilé
Et la terre s'est recouverte
De ta chair claire et je me suis senti léger
Tu es venue la solitude était vaincue
J'avais un guide sur la terre je savais
Me diriger je me savais démesuré
J'avançais je gagnais de l'espace et du temps

Death Love Life

I believed I could break the depths the immensity
By my grief stark naked without contact without echo
I stretched myself in my prison with virgin gates
Like a reasonable corpse who knew how to die
A dead man uncrowned except by his nothingness
I stretched myself on the absurd waves
Of poison absorbed by the love of ash
Solitude seemed to me more lively than blood

I wanted to sever life
I wanted to share death with death
Return my heart to the void and the void to life
Erase everything until there was nothing neither pane nor vapor
Nor anything before or after wholly nothing
I had eliminated the ice of joined hands
I had eliminated the wintery frame
Of the vow to live that annuls itself.

You arrived the fire was then rekindled
The shadow surrendered cold from below lit up with stars
And the earth was recovered
By your clear flesh and I felt myself light
You came solitude was conquered
I had a guide on earth I knew
How to direct myself I knew myself to be beyond measure
I advanced I gained space and time

J'allais vers toi j'allais sans fin vers la lumière
La vie avait un corps l'espoir tendait sa voile
Le sommeil ruisselait de rêves et la nuit
Promettait à l'aurore des regards confiants
Les rayons de tes bras entrouvraient le brouillard
Ta bouche était mouillée des premières rosées
Le repos ébloui remplaçait la fatigue.
Et j'adorais l'amour comme à mes premiers jours.

Les champs sont labourés les usines rayonnent
Et le blé fait son nid dans une houle énorme
La moisson la vendange ont des témoins sans nombre
Rien n'est simple ni singulier
La mer est dans les yeux du ciel ou de la nuit
La forêt donne aux arbres la sécurité
Et les murs des maisons ont une peau commune
Et les routes toujours se croisent.

Les hommes sont faits pour s'entendre
Pour se comprendre pour s'aimer
Ont des enfants qui deviendront pères des hommes
Ont des enfants sans feu ni lieu
Qui réinventeront les hommes
Et la nature et leur patrie
Celle de tous les hommes
Celle de tous les temps.

I went toward you I went endlessly toward light
Life had a body hope stretched its sail
Sleep streamed with dreams and night
Promised confident gazes to dawn
The rays of your arms set the fog ajar
Your mouth was moistened by the first dews
Dazzled rest replaced fatigue
And I adored love as in my first days.

The fields are plowed the factories beam
And wheat makes its nest in an enormous swell
The harvest the vintage have witnesses without number
Nothing is simple or singular
The sea is in the eyes of the sky or of the night
The forest gives security to the trees
And the walls of the houses have a communal skin
And the roads always intersect.

Men are made to come to agreement
To understand to love each other
Have children who become fathers of men
Have children without hearth or place
Who will reinvent men
And nature and homeland
That of all men
That of all times.

Chanson

Dans l'amour la vie a encore
L'eau pure de ses yeux d'enfant
Sa bouche est encore une fleur
Qui s'ouvre sans savoir comment

Dans l'amour la vie a encore
Ses mains agrippantes d'enfant
Ses pieds partent de la lumière
Et ils s'en vont vers la lumière

Dans l'amour la vie a toujours
Un coeur léger et renaissant
Rien n'y pourra jamais finir
Demain s'y allège d'hier.

Song

In love life still holds
Pure water of its childlike eyes
Its mouth is still a flower
That opens without knowing how

In love life still owns
Its grasping child's hands
Its feet start from light
And they leave toward light

In love life has always
A light and renewing heart
Nothing within it will ever end
Here tomorrow casts off yesterday.

Il faut bien y croire

Les jeux de ces curieux enfants qui sont les nôtres
Jeux simples qui leur font les yeux émerveillés
Pleins d'une fièvre qui les rapproche et les éloigne
Du monde où nous rêvons de faire place aux autres

Les jeux d'azur et de nuages
De gentillesses et de courses à la mesure d'un coeur futur
Qui ne sera jamais coupable
Les yeux de ces enfants qui sont nos yeux anciens

Nous eûmes plus de charmes que jamais les fées.

One Must Really Believe It

The games of these odd children who are ours
Simple games which fill their eyes with wonder
Full of a fever that draws them near and distances them
From the world where we dream of making room for others

Games of azure and of clouds
Of kindnesses and races to the measure of a future heart
That will never be guilty
The eyes of these children which are our ancient eyes

We had more charms than ever the fays.

D'une bête

J'aime les bêtes c'est Maïakowski
Qui dit j'aime les bêtes et il a aussitôt envie
De le prouver il leur sourit et il les voit répondre

Nous avions une chienne elle était un peu folle
La tête un peu trop noire pour un corps trop gris
Il a fallu la tuer j'entends car c'est la chasse
A tout moment le coup de feu qui la consume

La source de la vie se courbe sur sa fin
Nous nous courbons chaque jour un peu plus
Sur notre chienne absente note chienne exigeante.

About an Animal

I love animals it is Mayakovsky
Who says I love animals and immediately he wants
To prove it he smiles at them and he sees them respond

We had a bitch she was a little crazy
The head a little too black for a body too grey
They had to kill her I hear because that's the hunt
At every moment the shot that consumes her

The source of life bends upon its end
We bend each day a little more
To our absent bitch our demanding bitch.

Et un sourire

La nuit n'est jamais complète
Il y a toujours puisque je le dis
Puisque je l'affirme
Au bout du chagrin une fenêtre ouverte
Une fenêtre éclairée
Il y a toujours un rêve qui veille
Désir à combler faim à satisfaire
Un coeur généreux
Une main tendue une main ouverte
Des yeux attentifs
Une vie la vie à se partager.

Sérénité

Mes sommets étaient à ma taille
J'ai roulé dans tous mes ravins
Et je suis bien certain que ma vie est banale
Mes amours ont poussé dans un jardin commun
Mes vérités et mes erreurs
J'ai pu les peser comme on pèse
Le blé qui double le soleil
Ou bien celui qui manque aux granges
J'ai donné à ma soif l'ombre d'un gouffre lourd
J'ai donné à ma joie de comprendre la forme
D'une jarre parfaite.

And a Smile

Night is never complete
There is forever since I say it
Since I affirm it
At the end of grief an open window
A lighted window
There is always a dream which stays awake
Desire to fill hunger to satisfy
A generous heart
A hand extended an open hand
Attentive eyes
A life the life to share.

Serenity

My peaks were made to my scale
I rolled in all my ravines
I am very sure that my life is banal
My loves have grown in a common garden
My truths and my errors
I have been able to weigh them as one weighs
The wheat which doubles the sun
Or rather that which is missing from the granges
I have given the shadow of a heavy abyss to my thirst
I have given my joy to understand the form
Of a perfect jar.

Matines

J'ai rêvé d'une grande route
Où tu étais seule à passer
L'oiseau blanchi par la rosée
S'éveillait à tes premiers pas

Dans la forêt verte et mouillée
S'ouvraient la bouche et l'oeil de l'aube
Toutes le feuilles s'allumaient
Tu commençais une journée

Rien ne devait faire long feu
Ce jour brillait comme tant d'autres
Je dormais j'étais né d'hier
Toi tu t'étais levée très tôt

Pour matinale m'accorder
Une perpétuelle enfance.

Matins

I dreamed of a great road
Where you alone passed by
The bird whitened by dew
Awoke at your first steps

In the green and damp forest
Opened the mouth and eye of dawn
All the leaves kindled
You began a day

Nothing should hang fire
This day shone like so many others
I slept I was born yesterday
Yourself you arose very early

Creature of dawn to grant me
A perpetual childhood.

Marine

Je te regarde et le soleil grandit
Il va bientôt couvrir notre journée
Eveille-toi coeur et couleur en tête
Pour dissiper les malheurs de la nuit

Je te regarde tout est nu
Dehors les barques ont peu d'eau
Il faut tout dire en peu de mots
La mer est froide sans amour

C'est le commencement du monde
Les vagues vont bercer le ciel
Toi tu te berces dans tes draps
Tu tires le sommeil à toi

Eveille-toi que je suive tes traces
J'ai un corps pour t'attendre pour te suivre
Des portes de l'aube aux portes de l'ombre
Un corps pour passer ma vie à t'aimer

Un coeur pour rêver hors de ton sommeil.

Seascape

I look at you and the sun grows
Soon it will cover our day
Wake up heart and color first
Dissolve night's sorrows

I look at you everything is bare
Outside the boats are in low tide
Everything must be said in few words
The sea is cold without love

It is the beginning of the world
The waves are going to rock the sky
You rock yourself in your sheets
You pull sleep toward you

Wake up so that I may follow your tracks
I have a body to wait to follow you
From the doors of dawn to the doors of shadow
A body to spend my life loving you

A heart to dream outside your sleep.

Marilyn Kallet is the author of eleven other books, including *Circe, After Hours,* poetry from BkMk Press/UMKC; with Judith Ortiz Cofer, she co-edited *Sleeping With One Eye Open: Women Writers and the Art of Survival,* University of Georgia Press. She received her M.A. and Ph.D. in Comparative Literature from Rutgers University, and studied at the Sorbonne. Marilyn Kallet holds the Hodges Chair for Distinguished Teaching in English at the University of Tennessee.

This book was prepress-produced by Nancy C. Hanger.

All Black Widow Press titles are printed on acid-free paper and bound into a sewn & glued binding. Manufactured in the United States of America.

www.blackwidowpress.com

This book was set in Adobe's Cronos Pro, designed by Robert Slimbach as a modern sans serifed type based on oldstyle roman letterforms, and Monotype's Bell, designed in 1931, often called the first Modern English typeface. The titling font is Aculida, a modernistic typeface used by many of the Dadaists in their typographic artworks.

typeset & designed by Windhaven Press
www.windhaven.com

green
press
INITIATIVE

Black Widow Press is committed to preserving ancient forests and natural resources. We elected to print *Last Love Poems Of Paul Eluard* on 50% post consumer recycled paper, processed chlorine free. As a result, for this printing, we have saved:

9 Trees (40' tall and 6-8" diameter)
3,591 Gallons of Waste Water
1,444 Kilowatt Hours of Electricity
396 Pounds of Solid Waste
778 Pounds of Greenhouse Gases

Black Widow Press made this paper choice because our printer, Thomson-Shore, Inc., is a member of Green Press Initiative, a nonprofit program dedicated to supporting authors, publishers, and suppliers in their efforts to reduce their use of fiber obtained from endangered forests.

For more information, visit www.greenpressinitiative.org